#180⁰⁰

D0687913

The Mini - Encyclopedia of

PUBLIC DOMAIN SONGS

MUS*LIB
ML
13
Z56
1999

The BZ/Rights Stuff, Inc.
121 W. 27th St., Suite 901, New York, NY 10001
Phone: (212) 924-3000
Fax: (212) 924-2525

The musical compositions in this book are in the Public Domain in the United States only. Other countries have different rules about Public Domain.

PROPERTY OF EL CAMINO COLLEGE
MUSIC LIBRARY

This book is published by The BZ/Rights Stuff, Inc.,
a subsidiary of
BZ/Rights & Permissions, Inc., 121 West 27th St., Suite 901, New York,
N.Y. 10001

The Mini-Encyclopedia of Public Domain Songs
Copyright ©1993, 1994, 1995, 1996, 1997, 1998, 1999
by The BZ/Rights Stuff, Inc.

This publication is a creative work copyrighted by The BZ/Rights Stuff,
Inc. and fully protected by all applicable copyright laws, as well as by
misappropriation, trade secret, unfair competition and other applicable
laws. The authors and editors of this work have added value to the
underlying factual material herein through one or more of the following:
unique and original selection, coordination, expression, arrangement,
and classification of the information. The BZ/Rights Stuff, Inc. will
vigorously defend all of its rights in this publication. All rights reserved.
No part of this publication may be reproduced, stored in a retrieval
system, or transmitted in any form, by any means, digital, electronic,
mechanical, photocopying, recording or otherwise without permission of
The BZ/Rights Stuff, Inc.

ISBN 1-884286-00-3

Manufactured in the United States of America.

ABOUT THE AUTHOR

This reference work was compiled by copyright expert, Barbara Zimmerman, President of BZ/Rights & Permissions, Inc., and The BZ/Rights Stuff, Inc., a subsidiary. She learned the business from the ground up, by dealing with copyright and clearance issues in production, theater, book and music publishing, recordings, radio shows, commercials and all sorts of educational projects.

In the late 70's, she founded BZ/Rights & Permissions, Inc. It was among the first, and is among the best-known, of the independent rights' clearance services.

Her service clears rights for music, recordings, film and video footage, written materials, photographs, art work/graphics, cartoon characters—and celebrities— anything that's copyrighted or otherwise legally protected. Public Domain has always been an area of special interest and expertise for her.

The service's client list runs the gamut from AT&T, BBDO Worldwide, Encyclopaedia Britannica, IBM, General Motors, McCann-Erickson, McDonald's, McGraw-Hill, Ogilvy & Mather, Time-Warner, and Young & Rubicam, to filmmakers Spike Lee and Whit Stillman, to name only a few.

Ms. Zimmerman is a frequent speaker and writer on the subject of rights clearance and Public Domain. She has been a speaker for Seybold, E3, ITVA (International Television Association), IICS, The CD-ROM Convention, New York University, Association of Independent FilmMakers, New York Women In Film, New School for Social Research and The Ad Age Creative Workshop. Her articles have been published in Publishers Weekly, AV/Video, Software Publishing Association News, CD-ROM Professional, Photomethods, Video Systems, New Media and Videography.

ABOUT THE MINI-ENCYCLOPEDIA

The musical compositions in this book are in the Public Domain in the United States only. Other countries have different rules about Public Domain.

You _must_ read and understand the _"Important Cautions"_, directly following "About The Mini-Encyclopedia," before using any of the songs that are listed in this reference work.

The Mini-Encyclopedia is arranged in four parts:

1) A listing of all the songs in alphabetical order by title, including the date the song was written—followed by the writers' and composers' names and their birth and death dates, any special notes and an indication of whether the song was used in a theatrical performance or a film.

2) A listing of all the songs by category, directly following the alphabetical listing of songs. Many songs appear in more than one category. The categories are:

Blues Selections
Children's Songs
Christmas Selections
Classical Selections
Folksongs
Inspirational Songs
International Favorites
Love Songs
Marches
Patriotic Songs (includes songs associated with wars)
Place Names in Songs
Popular Songs
Silent Film Era Songs
Special Occasion Songs (birthday, graduation, wedding, etc.)
Spirituals
Tangos
Waltzes

3) If four or more titles by one composer appear in the alphabetical title listing at the front of the book, they are listed in this section under the composer's name.

4) A list of all the composers with their birth and death dates.

Key to Abbreviations Used in *The Mini-Encyclopedia*

w.	Words
m.	Music
w.m.	Words and Music
(M)	In a musical theatrical production
(F)	In a film

The name of the show or film follows directly after (M) or (F). *Example*:

Be My Little Baby Bumble Bee (1912) w. Stanley Murphy (1875-1919 A)
      m. Henry I. Marshall (1883-1958). (M) The Ziegfeld Follies of 1911
      (F) Hoppity Goes to Town, By the Light of the Silvery Moon

This indicates that the song was in a musical called, "The Ziegfeld Follies of 1911" and in two movies, *Hoppity Goes to Town* and *By the Light of the Silvery Moon.*

We've tried to list most of the well-known shows or films in which a song appeared.

Words in bold in parenthesis before or after a song title are included in order to help with your identification of a particular song. They usually indicate one of three things:

1) A recognizable lyric line from a song. *Example*:

Battle Hymn of the Republic (Glory, glory hallelujah) (1861/62)
w. Julia Ward Howe (1819-1910) m. (?) same as "John Brown's Body"

2) An alternate title for that song. *Example:*

Jimmy Crack Corn (The Blue Tail Fly) (1846) Traditional American

3) Other words in the title. The song has come to be known by a shorter title.
Examples:

Hot Time in the Old Town Tonight (There'll Be a) (1896) w. Joseph Hayden
      (? -1937) m. Theodore A. Metz (1848-1936). (M) Me and Bessie

(In My Sweet Little) Alice Blue Gown (1919) w. Joseph McCarthy (1885-1943)
      m. Harry Tierney (1890-1965). (M) Irene (F) Irene

How the songs in *The Mini-Encyclopedia* were selected

This listing of Public Domain (PD for short) songs does not claim to be all-inclusive. Thousands of songs and other musical works have fallen into the Public Domain over the years. Most musical works that are PD are of little value because people aren't familiar with the words or the music.

What we have tried to create in this Mini-Encyclopedia is a _very selective_ listing of songs and other musical works that most people recognize the minute they hear them. These are familiar melodies; well-loved songs; songs that strike a chord of memory; musical works that are usable in *what you are producing right now*—whether it's a commercial, a feature film, a TV show or any other project you may have in mind.

Notes about the songs

Any special notes or observations made about these songs appear to the right of their titles in the A to Z list. They are not repeated in the list by category. *Example:* Beside "A-Tisket A-Tasket" is the notation that the children's rhyme is PD—but the Ella Fitzgerald version of this song is not. (While we cannot guarantee to have commented on everything of this nature, we have tried to do so when we were aware of problems with a particular song.)

GATT: Restoration of copyright under GATT which began on January 1, 1996 does not apply to any song in the ***Mini-Encyclopedia.*** All of the songs in the ***Mini-Encyclopedia*** have completed their full term of copyright under the U.S. Copyright Law.

Dating of Songs and Birth and Death Dates of Composers

We are now listing, whenever possible, birth and death dates for composers and a year of origin for each piece of music.

The composers' death dates will be of great value to anyone trying to determine the copyright status of these compositions throughout the world.

About the composer's birth and death dates

Composers' death dates may be found in two places: 1) Directly after the composer's name in each selection listing; 2) in the alphabetical listing of composers at the end of the book after song categories.

As you probably know, most countries have no official national death registry. Therefore, we have had to use various secondary sources, such as reference books and resources like ASCAP, BMI, MCPS and PRS to document the composers' death dates. All the dates provided in *The Mini-Encyclopedia* are based on: 1) more than one reliable source agreeing on the dates; 2) one source, if that source was an obituary in a recognized newspaper; 3) in addition, because dates are so necessary to determine world-wide copyright status, we have also listed dates obtained solely from the performing rights societies: ASCAP, BMI, PRS, MCPS, etc. We have indicated these single-source dates by placing an initial after the date to indicate which society supplied it.

Example: (1895-1942 A) indicates the date was supplied by ASCAP.
Example: (? -1945 P) indicates that the date was supplied by PRS, which keeps track of death dates only.

For more information about what the letters stand for, see the end of this section .

Questionable birth dates are indicated with: ?, but in no case is a ? given for a death date. We may indicate that a death date is uncertain by supplying two dates, such as: 1944/45 — which means we are not sure if the composer died in 1944 or 1945 but that our sources agree that it is one year or the other.

No death date at all means one of two things: (a) the composer is still alive or (b) we have not been able to verify a death date thoroughly enough to include it.

> *We have taken as much care as possible to provide complete and accurate dates, but for all of the above reasons, we cannot warrant their accuracy.*

About the dates given for when the compositions were written, published, copyrighted or performed

This reference work's very existence is predicated on the fact that we guarantee that all the compositions in it are in the Public Domain in the United States. It has not been possible to locate an absolute date for every composition. We indicated our inability to supply the precise year a composition was written in the following ways:

1) We may simply cite a composition as being written in the 1700's—meaning that all of our reference sources indicate it was written sometime in the 1700's, but they could not agree on a specific date.

2) By simply identifying a composition as Traditional. Most traditional pieces do not have a date for the year they were written, as the essence of a traditional piece is that it has been around for many years, has had many changes, and that its date of origin and composers are simply not known with any accuracy.

3) By indicating what we think is the most likely date, followed by a question mark. For example, "American Patrol (1885?)" means that we think the composition was written around 1885, as most of our reference sources agree on that year for the date of the composition, but that the sources disagree slightly.

4) By using two dates. "Washington Post March," for instance, seems to have had its band parts copyrighted in 1889, according to one reputable source. But another reputable source says that the piece was also registered for copyright, in some other form, in 1893. So our listing says: (1889/93).

5) In dating classical works and a few other early works composed before 1900, we found that some reference books date the work by first performance, others by the date the music was first written or published, and still others by the date it was registered for copyright (if it was registered for copyright at all). So there can be a wide variance on dates for early works, depending on what reference book is being consulted. No scholarly effort to determine what might be the more "correct" date was made, as all the possible dates put the selection firmly in the Public Domain in the United States. And that is our only concern in creating this reference work. Again, regardless of question marks, terms like "Traditional," or broad indications for dating like "the 1700's," every piece of music in this reference work is in the Public Domain in the United States.

Explanation of Symbols and Notations Used in Conjunction With Dates

Example: **Roses of Picardy** (1916) w. Frederick E. Weatherly (1848-1929)
 m. Haydn Wood (? -1959 P). American song popular during World War I; Picardy is a region in France.

The date after the title is the date the composition was written. The dates after each composer's name are birth and death dates. Haydn Wood's dates indicate that we do not know when he was born and that his death date, 1959, is confirmed only by PRS.

If there is no death date, we believe that the composer is alive and his/her date would appear as follows: (1924-   )

No birth date (meaning no one is sure when the composer was born) is indicated with a "?", ex: (?-1959). Often we have no birth dates because the performance societies only keep track of death dates.

The notation: (date of birth?-living per BMI) means that the composer is alive as of this edition, and is currently a member of BMI; however, BMI is unable to provide a birth date for that composer.

A date provided by a performing rights society is indicated as follows:

A after the date for ASCAP   *Ex:* Maurice Abrahams (1883-1931 A)
B after the date for BMI   *Ex:* Robert Byrd (1930-1990 B)
M after the date for MCPS   *Ex:* James J. Russell (? -1900 M)
P after the date for PRS   *Ex:* Guy d'Hardelot (? -1936 P)
S after the date for SIAE   *Ex:* E. di Capua (1864-1917 S)
SA after the date for SADAIC   *Ex:* A.G. Villoldo (? -1919 SA)

A date confirmed by two performing rights societies is indicated with two initials.
        Ex: (? -1949 A & P) Both ASCAP and PRS have this death date in their records.

If there is no death date after a composer's name, it means one of two things:
a) we have not been able to verify a death date thoroughly enough to include it or
b) the composer is still alive.

Important Cautions

These works are in the Public Domain in the United States <u>only</u>. Other countries have different rules about Public Domain.*

Before you use this list you *must* read the following cautions. Although all the songs on this list are in the Public Domain, there are a number of important legal issues that come into play that you must pay attention to when you are dealing with Public Domain materials.

This listing is not intended as legal advice; but as a research tool.

1) **TITLES** - Titles of songs cannot be copyrighted. However, they may be protected legally in other ways. It is therefore possible to have many songs with the same title. For instance, there are probably 300 songs titled "Because" by 300 different sets of writers and composers. Thus, when we tell you a song is in the Public Domain on this list, we do not mean that *any* song by that title is in the Public Domain, we mean the song written by the writers and composers we list by the title, is in the Public Domain. **To correctly identify a Public Domain song you must have the correct title by the correct writers and composers.**

2) **RECORDINGS** - Recordings of these songs are <u>not</u> in the Public Domain. Although the words and music of the songs on the attached list are in the Public Domain, when a music company makes a recording, it owns that recording of the song. So if you want to use an already recorded version of the song—an existing recording, whether on an LP, cassette, tape or CD purchased at a music store or that you or a friend have at home—**you need permission from the company that produced the recording to do so.**

If you want to make your own recording of the words and music of the song in a studio with your own musicians and talent, you do not need permission from anyone as long as you use the original Public Domain version of the song and your own arrangement.

* If you need to be sure that the song you are choosing is in the Public Domain throughout the world, The BZ/Rights Stuff can help you. Call the number listed on the title page of this book.

3) **ARRANGEMENTS** - Under the United States' copyright law, you can copyright an arrangement of a Public Domain song separately from the song itself. That means **it is possible to have a copyrighted arrangement of a Public Domain song** (an arrangement that legally belongs to someone). In using these songs, you must avoid using anyone's copyrighted arrangement and only use the song as originally written by the writers and composers listed beside the title, or create your own arrangement of the song.

Here are two examples of copyrighted arrangements: 1) "America the Beautiful," with words by Katherine Lee Bates and music by Samuel Augustus Ward, was written in 1895 and is in the Public Domain. However, the recording of the song made famous by Ray Charles is a **copyrighted arrangement** that he has written. If you use his arrangement, you need to get permission from his music publisher and pay the music publisher a fee. 2) A classical selection written in the 1800's can have a current copyrighted orchestral arrangement. To use that copyrighted arrangement, you would need permission from the music publisher that owns it.

If you need to locate a true PD version of a musical composition, it should have a copyright notice of **1922 or before**. How do you obtain a copy of a piece of music as originally written? Try your public library or a large music store that carries sheet music. Dover Publications, located in Mineola, N.Y., publishes a lot of Public Domain sheet music.

4) **SOMEONE WRITES NEW COPYRIGHTED LYRICS TO AN OLD MELODY -** "Waves of the Danube" was written in 1880. In 1947, Al Jolson and Saul Chaplin wrote words to this music and titled the song, "Anniversary Song." The melody of "Waves of the Danube" is in the Public Domain—the words to it written by Jolson and Chaplin are **not** Public Domain. Thus you will find "Waves of the Danube" on this Public Domain list but you will not see "Anniversary Song."

John Philip Sousa wrote his marches in the late 1800's. People have since put words to them. The Sousa marches as he wrote them are in the Public Domain. The new words aren't.

5) **SONGS WRITTEN IN A FOREIGN LANGUAGE** - If the song is listed in its original language, it is in the Public Domain in **that** language. "Un Bel Di," from *Madama Butterfly,* is in the Public Domain in Italian. If you use an English translation of the song, you must make sure that the translation is in the Public Domain. Translations into other languages can be copyrighted. An excellent example is that while the great Greek plays are in the Public Domain in Greek, the famous English translations by Lattimore, Fitts and Fitzgerald are covered by the Copyright Law. One solution to this problem is to do your own translation—and then you own it.

6) **TRADITIONAL SONGS -** The origins of old songs like "Shenandoah" or "On Top of Old Smokey" are often lost in time or date back to the 1600's, 1700's or 1800's. However, many have been recorded by popular singers years later, using copyrighted arrangements, with new or different words added. If you are using a traditional song, you must be careful to use it in its original form, and not a modern update. Sheet music for such songs is usually printed with the notation "Traditional" or "Folksong" or "Anonymous" where the composer's name would be. If you obtain a piece of sheet music that credits writers and composers or arrangers or contains a copyright notice, it is probably **not** a Public Domain version of the traditional song.

7) **A GENERAL RULE ABOUT THIS LIST - <u>You must use the songs listed in the Mini-Encyclopedia as they were written by the writers and composers noted by the title of each song on this list</u>**. A different writer or composer's name or an *additional* writer or composer's name may indicate the author of a copyrighted arrangement, the writer of new words set to an old melody, or the composer of a new version of a traditional song. If the version of the song you are using is not credited only to the writers and composers exactly as we list them, **the song may not be in the Public Domain.**

If you have purchased this reference work and feel you need a further explanation of any of these concepts, you are welcome to call The BZ/Rights Stuff, Inc. in New York City at 212-924-3000 for a fuller explanation or to ask any questions you may have— at no charge.

LOOKING FOR PUBLIC DOMAIN TITLES THAT ARE NOT LISTED HERE?

As noted before, one of the major criteria for including songs on this list is that they are well-known titles. What if you are looking for not-so-well-known titles, or a particular genre of music? For instance, a list of World War I songs that were popular at the time? Lesser-known songs that Jerome Kern or Irving Berlin wrote, that are in the Public Domain? A list of Civil War songs? Or even a list of literature that's in the Public Domain?

We Can Help. Call us at 212-924-3000.

Proper and legal use of this listing of Public Domain selections is subject to the limitations discussed on the preceding pages, entitled "Important Cautions."

These works are in the Public Domain in the United States <u>only</u>. Other countries have different rules about Public Domain.

A-Hunting We Will Go Traditional song usually considered a children's song

A-Tisket A-Tasket Traditional children's nursery rhyme. *The Ella Fitzgerald version of this song is* **not** *Public Domain.*

Aba Daba Honeymoon, The (1914) w.m. Arthur Fields (1888-1953), Walter Donovan (1888-1964 A). (F) Two Weeks with Love

Abide with Me (Fast falls the eventide) (1840/60) w. Henry Francis Lyte (1793-1847) m. William Henry Monk (1823-1889)

Ach (O) Du Lieber Augustin (Polly [Molly] Put the Kettle On) (Did You Ever See a Lassie?) (m. 1788/89? w. 1800?)

Adeste Fideles (O Come All Ye Faithful) (1700's) Traditional Christmas carol. w. Latin: John Francis Wade (1710/11-1786) w. English: Frederick Oakeley (1802-1880) m. John Francis Wade (1710/11-1786)

After the Ball (1892) w.m. Charles K. Harris (1867-1930). (M) A Trip to Chinatown

After You've Gone (1918) w.m. Henry Creamer (1879-1930), Turner Layton (1894-1978). (M) Me and Bessie (F) For Me and My Gal, Jolson Sings Again, Unholy Partners

Ah! So Pure (1848) From the opera, "Martha." w. W. Friedrich m. Friedrich von Flotow (1812/13-1883)

Ah! Sweet Mystery of Life (1910) w. Rida Johnson Young (1869-1926) m. Victor Herbert (1859-1924). (M) Naughty Marietta (F) Naughty Marietta, The Great Victor Herbert

Aida (1871/72) Opera. w. A. Ghislanzoni (1824-1893) m. Giuseppe Verdi (1813-1901)

Ain't We Got Fun (1921) w. Gus Kahn (1886-1941), Raymond B. Egan (1890-1952) m. Richard A. Whiting (1891-1938). (F) By the Light of the Silvery Moon, I'll See You in My Dreams

Air for the G String (1729/31) From Orchestral Suite No. 3. m. J. S. Bach (1685-1750)

Alexander's Ragtime Band (1911) w.m. Irving Berlin (1888-1989). (M) Hullo Ragtime (F) Alexander's Ragtime Band, There's No Business Like Show Business

(In My Sweet Little) Alice Blue Gown (1919) w. Joseph McCarthy (1885-1943) m. Harry Tierney (1890-1965). (M) Irene (F) Irene

All By Myself (1921) w.m. Irving Berlin (1888-1989). (F) Blue Skies

All Through the Night (1784) Anonymous Welsh

Aloha Oe (1800's) Hawaiian. w.m. Princess Liliuokalani (1838-1917). (F) Aloha

Along the Rocky Road to Dublin (1915) w. Joe Young (1889-1939) m. Bert Grant (1878-1951 A)

Alouette (probably 1879) Anonymous French-Canadian. (F) People Are Funny

Alphabet Song (A, b, c, d, etc.) Traditional children's song. w. Anonymous m. Same as "Twinkle, Twinkle, Little Star," "Baa, Baa, Black Sheep."

Also Sprach Zarathustra (1885/96) Symphonic poem. m. Richard Strauss (1864-1949). (F) 2001: A Space Odyssey

Amazing Grace Traditional. *Make sure you use the traditional version written around 1799/1800, not a modern version of this song.*

America (My country 'tis of thee) (m. 1700's/ w. 1831/32) w. Samuel Francis Smith (1808-1895) m. Same as "God Save the King".

America the Beautiful (1895) w. Katharine Lee Bates (1859-1929) m. Samuel Augustus Ward (1847/8-1903). (F) The Bells of Capistrano, With a Song in My Heart

American Patrol (1885?) m. F.W. Meacham (1850/56-1909). (F) Orchestra Wives, The Glenn Miller Story. *Only the instrumental music of this selection is in the Public Domain. In the 1940's, "We Must Be Vigilant," words by Edgar Leslie (1885-1976) and music adapted by Joseph Burke, was sung to this melody. "We Must Be Vigilant" is* **not** *Public Domain.*

Anchors Aweigh (1906) m. Charles A. Zimmerman (1861/62-1916). *The music for "Anchors Aweigh" is definitely in the Public Domain. There are questions about the origin of the lyrics, so you need to be careful about using any lyrics. If you are using lyrics, you should use lyrics that were published 76 years ago or more.*

And the Green Grass Grew All Around (1912) w. William Jerome (1865-1932 A) m. Harry von Tilzer (1872-1946)

Angels from the Realms of Glory Traditional Christmas carol. w. James Montgomery (1771-1854) m. Henry Smart (1813-1879)

Angels We Have Heard on High Traditional Christmas carol

Annie Laurie (1830's) Scottish. w. William Douglas m. Lady John Scott

Anvil Chorus (1853) From the opera, "Il Trovatore." w. Salvatore Cammarano (1801-1852) m. Giuseppe Verdi (1813-1901)

Apache Dance – Offenbach (1861) m. J. Offenbach (1819-1880)

April Showers (1921) w. Bud (B.G.) De Sylva (1895-1950) m. Louis Silvers (1889-1954). (F) The Jolson Story, April Showers, Jolson Sings Again, The Eddy Duchin Story

Are You Sleeping (Frère Jacques) (1800's) Traditional French children's song

Arkansas Traveler, The (1800's) Traditional American

Artist's Life (1867) m. Johann Strauss, Jr. (1825-1899)

Asleep in the Deep (1897) w. Arthur J. Lamb (1870-1928) m. Henry W. Petrie (1857-1925)

Assembly (Bugle Call) (There's a monkey in the grass) (1842) American

Au Clair de la Lune (Mon ami, Pierrot) (1811) Traditional French

Auf Wiedersehen (1915) w. Herbert Reynolds (1867-1933) m. Sigmund Romberg (1887-1951). (M) The Blue Paradise (F) Deep in My Heart

Auld Lang Syne (1700's) Traditional New Year's Eve song. w. Robert Burns (1759-1796) m. Traditional

Avalon (1920) w. Al Jolson (1886-1950), Bud (B.G.) De Sylva (1895-1950) m. Vincent Rose **or** w.m. Al Jolson, Vincent Rose (1880-1944), arrangement by J. Bodewalt Lampe (1869-1929 A). *The 1920 arrangement by Lampe is in the Public Domain in the United States. This song is based on Puccini's aria "E lucevan le stelle" from "Tosca."*

Ave Maria (Bach/Gounod) (Bach 1735/38/42 / Gounod 1859) w. Bible: Luke 1:28 w. French: Paul Bernard m. Charles Gounod (1818-1893). Gounod superimposed an original melody over J.S. Bach's (1685-1750) C-Major Prelude from "The Well-Tempered Clavier."

Ave Maria (Schubert) (1826) w. Walter Scott (1771-1832) m. Franz Schubert (1797-1828)

Away in a Manger (1800's) Traditional Christmas carol. w. Anonymous m. James Ramsey Murray (1841-1905)

Baa, Baa, Black Sheep Traditional children's song. w. Anonymous m. Same tune as "Twinkle, Twinkle, Little Star," "Alphabet Song."

Babes in the Wood (1915) w. Schuyler Greene (1880-1927 A), Jerome Kern (1885-1945) m. Jerome Kern (1885-1945). (M) Very Good Eddie

Baby Bunting Traditional children's song

Baby Shoes (1916) w. Joe Goodwin (1889-1943 A), Ed Rose (1875-1935) m. Al Piantadosi (1884-1955)

Baby Won't You Please Come Home (1919) w.m. Charles Warfield, Clarence Williams (1893/98-1965). (F) That's The Spirit

(Back Home Again in) Indiana (1917) w. Ballard MacDonald (1882-1935 A) m. James F. Hanley (1892-1942 A). (F) With a Song in My Heart, Satchmo the Great, Drum Crazy, The Five Pennies

Ballin' the Jack (1913) w. James Henry Burris m. Chris Smith (1879-1949). (M) The Passing Show of 1915 (F) For Me and My Gal, On the Riviera, That's My Boy

Band Played On, The (Casey would waltz with a strawberry blonde) (1895) w. Charles B. Ward (1865-1917) m. John E. Palmer. (F) Lillian Russell, The Strawberry Blonde

Barcarolle (1864) From the opera, "The Tales of Hoffmann." w. J. Barbier (1822/25-1901) and M. Carré (?-1872), based on stories by E.T.A. Hoffmann m. Jacques Offenbach (1819-1880)

Battle Cry of Freedom (1863) w.m. George Frederick Root (1820-1895)

Battle Hymn of the Republic (Glory, glory hallelujah) (1861/62)
w. Julia Ward Howe (1819-1910) m. (?) same as "John Brown's Body"

Be My Little Baby Bumble Bee (1912) w. Stanley Murphy (1875-1919 A)
m. Henry I. Marshall (1883-1958). (M) The Ziegfeld Follies of 1911
(F) Hoppity Goes to Town, By the Light of the Silvery Moon

Beale Street (1916/17) w.m. W.C. Handy (1873-1958). (F) St. Louis Blues. *This song
was later copyrighted as "Beale Street Blues" with an arrangement by Henri
Klickmann. This later arrangement is **not** Public Domain. Use the song as written by
W.C. Handy in 1916.*

Beautiful Dreamer (1864) w.m. Stephen Foster (1826-1864). (F) Swanee River

Beautiful Isle of Somewhere (1897) w. Jessie Brown Pounds (1861-1921) m. John S.
Fearis (1867-1932)

Beautiful Ohio (1918) w. Ballard MacDonald (1882-1935 A) m. Mary Earl (1862/63-
1932) (Mary Earl is a pseudonym of Robert A. King)

Because (1898) w. Charles Horwitz (1864-1938) m. Frederick V. Bowers (1874-1961 A)

Because (1902) w. Edward Teschemacher (? -1940 P) m. Guy d'Hardelot (? -1936 P).
(F) Three Smart Girls Grow Up

Because You're You (1906) w. Henry Blossom (1866-1919) m. Victor Herbert
(1859-1924). (M) The Red Mill

Bedelia (1903) w. William Jerome (1865-1932 A) m. Jean Schwartz (1878-1956)

Believe Me If All Those Endearing Young Charms (1775/1807) w. Thomas
Moore (1779-1852) m. Traditional English-Irish-Scottish

Bells of St. Mary's, The (1917) w. Douglas Furber (1885/86-1961) m. A. Emmett Adams (? -1938 P). (F) The Bells of St. Mary's

Berceuse (1888) From the opera, "Jocelyn." w. Armand Silvestre (1837/8-1901), Victor Capoul (1839-1924) m. Benjamin Godard (1849-1895)

Bicycle Built for Two, A (Daisy Bell) (Daisy Daisy) (1892) w.m. Harry Dacre (? -1922 P). (F) I'll Be Your Sweetheart

Big Rock Candy Mountain (1885?) Traditional American. (F) Nighttime in Nevada

Bill Bailey, Won't You Please Come Home? (1902) w.m. Hughie Cannon (1877-1912). (F) The Five Pennies

Billy Boy (c.1824) Traditional children's song

Bimini Bay (1921) w. Gus Kahn (1886-1941), Raymond B. Egan (1890-1952) m. Richard A. Whiting (1891-1938)

Bingo Traditional children's game/song

Bird in a Gilded Cage, A (1900) w. Arthur J. Lamb (1870-1928) m. Harry von Tilzer (1872-1946). (F) Ringside Maisie

Blest Be the Tie That Binds (1782) w.m. John Fawcett (1739/40-1817), Hans G. Naegeli (1773-1836), Kurt Kaiser

Blow the Man Down (Late 1800's) Traditional American-British

Blue Bell of Scotland, The (1800's) Traditional Scottish

Blue Danube, The (1867) Waltz. m. Johann Strauss, Jr. (1825-1899) (F) 2001: A Space Odyssey

Blue Tail Fly, The (Jimmy Crack Corn) (1846) Traditional American

Boar's Head Carol, The Traditional Christmas carol

Bobby Shafto (c.1750) Traditional sea chantey

Bonnie Blue Flag, The (1861/62) w. Annie Chambers-Ketchum (1824?-1904)
m. Harry MacCarthy. Popular song of the Confederate States during the Civil War.

Boola, Boola (Yale Boola) (1901) Anonymous American. Based on "La Hoola Boola,"
(1898) by Robert (Bob) Cole (1869-1911) and Billy Johnson

Bourrée From "Water Music." (1749) m. George Frederick Handel (1685-1759)

Bourrée From "Royal Fireworks Music." (1715) m. George Frederick Handel (1685-1759)

Bowery, The (1892) w. Charles H. Hoyt (1860-1900) m. Percy Gaunt (1852-1896).
(M) A Trip to Chinatown (F) Sunbonnet Sue

Brandenburg Concertos (1718/21) m. J.S. Bach (1685-1750) Six Concertos.

Breeze from Alabama, A (1901/02) m. Scott Joplin (1868-1919)

Broadway Rose (1920) w. Eugene West (1883-1949 A) m. Martin Fried (1923-1980
A), Otis Spencer (1890-1958 A)

Bride Elect, The (1897/98) m. John Philip Sousa (1854-1932)

Britannia (Columbia), the Gem of the Ocean (1843) Reference books indicate that
it is unclear who wrote this selection.

By the Beautiful Sea (1914) w. Harold R. Atteridge (1886-1938) m. Harry Carroll
(1892-1962). (F) The Story of Vernon and Irene Castle, Some Like It Hot

By the Light of the Silvery Moon (1909) w. Edward Madden (1877-1952) m. Gus Edwards (1879-1945). (M) The Ziegfeld Follies (F) The Birth of the Blues, The Jolson Story, By the Light of the Silvery Moon

By the Waters of Minnetonka (1914) w. J.M. Cavanass m. Thurlow Lieurance (1878-1963)

Caissons Go Rolling Along, The (1918) w.m. Edmund L. Gruber (1879-1941). (F) Ice Capades Review, The Heat's On. *In 1956, this song was adapted by Harold W. Arberg as "The Army Goes (Marching) Rolling Along" and designated the official song of the U.S. Army. The Army song is **not** Public Domain.*

Calvary w.m. Louis Spohr (1784-1859)

Campbells Are Coming, The (1745) Traditional Scottish

Camptown Races, De (1850) w.m. Stephen Foster (1826-1864). (F) Swanee River, Colorado, I Dream of Jeannie

Can Can (1858) From the opera, "Orpheus in the Underworld." m. Jacques Offenbach (1819-1880)

Cantique de Noël (O Holy Night) (1847/58) Traditonal Christmas carol. w. French: Placide Cappeau (1808-1877) w. English: John Sullivan Dwight (1813/18-1893) m. Adolphe-Charles Adam (1803-1856)

Capitan, El (1896) March. m. John Philip Sousa (1854-1932)

Capriccio Espagnol (1887/88) Symphonic poem. m. Nikolai Rimsky-Korsakov (1844-1908) (Op. 34)

Capriccio Italien (1880) m. Peter I.Tchaikovsky (1840-1893)

Caprice Viennois (1910) m. Fritz Kreisler (1875-1962)

Carmen (1875) Opera. w. H. Meilhac (1831-1897), L. Halévy (1834-1908), after a story by Prosper Mérimée m. Georges Bizet (1838-1875). Famous arias: "Habanera," "Toreador Song"

Carolina in the Morning (1922) w. Gus Kahn (1886-1941) m. Walter Donaldson (1893-1947). (M) Passing Show of 1922 (F) The Dolly Sisters, April Showers, Jolson Sings Again, I'll See You in My Dreams

Carry Me Back to Old Virginny (1878) w.m. James A. Bland (1854-1911). (F) Hullabaloo

Casey Jones (1909) w. T. Lawrence Seibert m. Eddie Newton (F) Sunset in Wyoming

Chicago (That Toddling Town) (1922) w.m. Fred Fisher (1875-1942). (F) Oh You Beautiful Doll, With a Song in My Heart, The Joker Is Wild, The Story of Vernon and Irene Castle. *The 1922 arrangement by George Holman is in the Public Domain in the United States.*

Chicken Reel, The (1910) m. Joseph M. Daly (1888-1968 A). *This music is often used as the instrumental background for the Looney Tunes' chicken character, Foghorn Leghorn.*

Chinatown, My Chinatown (1906 or 1910) w. William Jerome (1865-1932 A) m. Jean Schwartz (1878-1956). (M) Up and Down Broadway, Push and Go (F) The Seven Little Foys, Is Everybody Happy?, Jolson Sings Again

Choclo, El (1911/13) Tango. w. (?) m. A.G. Villoldo (?-1919 SA). This song is a classic tango of Argentine origin. *The 1952 song, "Kiss of Fire" is based on this song, but "Kiss of Fire" is* **not** *Public Domain.*

Chopsticks (1877) m. Arthur de Lulli. Actual title: "The Celebrated Chop Waltz"

Christmas Oratorio (1734) w.m. J.S. Bach (1685-1750)

Christmas Wishes (1848) w. L.W. Simpson (1811-1883) m. Charles Wood (1807-1876)

Chrysanthemum, The (1904) m. Scott Joplin (1868-1919)

Ciribiribin (1898/99) w. Carlo Tiochet m. A. Pestalozza (1851-1934 S). (F) One Night of Love, Heaven Can Wait

Clair de Lune (1905) m. Claude Debussy (1862-1918)

Clementine (Oh, My Darling Clementine) (1884/85) Traditional American. *The 1960 Woody Harris adaptation of this song is* **not** *Public Domain.*

Cockles and Mussels ([Sweet] Molly Malone) Traditional Irish

Colonel Bogey March (1914/16) March. m. Kenneth J. Alford (1881-1945) (Kenneth J. Alford is a pseudonym of Major Frederick J. Ricketts). (F) The Bridge on the River Kwai

Columbia (Britannia), the Gem of the Ocean (1843). Reference books indicate that it is unclear who wrote this selection.

Come, Friends, Who Plough the Sea (1879/80) From the operetta, "The Pirates of Penzance." w. W.S. Gilbert (1836-1911) m. Arthur Sullivan (1842-1900). "Hail, Hail, the Gang's All Here" is based on this chorus.

Come, Josephine, in My Flying Machine (1910) w. Alfred Bryan (1871-1958 A) m. Fred Fisher (1875-1942). (F) The Story of Vernon and Irene Castle, Oh You Beautiful Doll

Come, Thou Almighty King (mid-1700's) w. Anonymous m. Felice de Giardini (1716-1796)

Come to the Fair (1917) w. Helen Taylor (?-1943) m. Easthope Martin (1882-1925 A)

Come Unto Me (1906 and 1917 versions) Traditional Black American. *Henry (aka Harry) Thacker (H.T.) Burleigh (1866/86-1949) did arrangements of many traditional spirituals and popularized them in the early decades of the 1900's. The arrangement of this song by H.T. Burleigh is in the Public Domain.*

Comin' Thro' the Rye (If a body meet a body) (1796) Traditional Scottish

Concerto for Piano (1873) m. Edvard Grieg (1843-1907)

Coriolan Overture (1807) m. Ludwig van Beethoven (1770-1827)

Coronation March (La Marche du Sacre) (1849) From the opera, "Le Prophète." m. Giacomo Meyerbeer (1791-1864)

Cosi Fan Tutte (1790) Opera. w. Lorenzo Da Ponte (1749-1838) m. W.A. Mozart (1756-1791)

Cotton Gin Reel (1820) Traditional American

Coventry Carol, The (Lully, Lullay) Traditional Christmas carol

Cowboy's Lament, The (Streets of Laredo) (1800's) Traditional American. (F) Streets of Laredo, Utah Wagon Train. *There is a 1948 version of this song, by Ray Evan and Jay Livingston, that is **not** Public Domain.*

Creation, The (1797/98) w. English: Text based on "Paradise Lost" by Milton. Author unknown. w. German: Gottfried van Swieten (1733-1803) m. Franz Joseph Haydn (1732-1809)

Cuddle Up a Little Closer, Lovey Mine (1908) w. Otto Harbach (1873-1963) m. Karl Hoschna (1877-1911). (M) The Three Twins (F) The Birth of the Blues, Is Everybody Happy?, On Moonlight Bay

Daddy Long Legs (1919) w. Sam M. Lewis (1885-1959), Joe Young (1889-1939) m. Harry Ruby (1895-1974)

Daddy's Little Girl (1905) w. Edward Madden (1877-1952) m. Theodore F. Morse (1873/74-1924)

Daisy Bell (A Bicycle Built for Two) (Daisy, Daisy) (1892) w.m. Harry Dacre (? -1922 P). (F) I'll Be Your Sweetheart

Dance of the Hours (1876) From the opera, "La Gioconda." m. Amilcare Ponchielli (1834-1886). (F) Fantasia. *In 1963, Alan Sherman based his song, "Hello Mudduh, Hello Faddah" on this music. Sherman's song is **not** Public Domain.*

Danny Boy (1913) w.m. Frederick Edward Weatherly (1848-1929), adapted from the traditional Irish song, "Londonderry Air"

Danube Waves (Waves of the Danube) (1880) Waltz. m. I. Ivanovici (1845-1902). *In 1947, Al Jolson and Saul Chaplin based their song, "Anniversary Song," for the film "The Jolson Story," on this music. "Anniversary Song" is **not** Public Domain.*

Daphnis et Chloé (1912) Ballet. m. Maurice Ravel (1875-1937)

Dardanella (1919) w. Fred Fisher (1875-1942) m. Felix Bernard (1897-1944), Johnny S. Black (1891-1936). (M) Afgar

Daring Young Man, The (On the Flying Trapeze) (1868) w. George Leybourne (? -1884 P) m. Alfred Lee

Darktown Strutters' Ball, The (1917) w.m. Shelton Brooks (1886-1975 A). (F) The Story of Vernon and Irene Castle, Broadway

Darling Nelly Gray (1856) w.m. Benjamin Russell Hanby (1833-1867)

Daughter of Rosie O'Grady, The (1918) w. Monty C. Brice (1891-1962) m. Walter Donaldson (1893-1947). (F) The Daughter of Rosie O'Grady

Dear Little Boy of Mine (1918) w. J. Keirn Brennan (1873-1948) m. Ernest R. Ball (1878-1927)

Dear Old Pal of Mine (1918) w. Harold Robé (1881-1946 A) m. Gitz Rice (1891-1947)

Deck the Halls (1784) Traditional Christmas carol. w. Anonymous American (?)
m. Traditional Welsh

Deep River Traditional Black American. *Henry (aka Harry) Thacker (H.T.) Burleigh
(1866/86-1949) did arrangements of many traditional spirituals and popularized them
in the early decades of the 1900's. The arrangement of this song done by H.T.
Burleigh is in the Public Domain.*

**Did You Ever See a Lassie? (O [Ach] Du Lieber Augustin) (Polly [Molly]
Put the Kettle On)** (m. 1788-89? w. 1909)

Ding Dong Bell Traditional Mother Goose children's song

Dixie (1860) w.m. Daniel Decatur Emmett (1815-1904). (F) With a Song in My Heart

Do It Again (1912) w.m. Irving Berlin (1888-1989)

Do It Some More (and more and more) (1912) w. Thomas Mack (1880-1943)
m. Charles Greene (1874-1937)

Don Giovanni (1801) Opera. w. Lorenzo Da Ponte (1749-1838) m. W.A. Mozart
(1756-1791)

Dona Nobis Pacem Traditional. w.m. Anonymous

Don't Go in the Lion's Cage Tonight (1906) w.m. E. Ray Goetz (1886-1954),
John Gilroy (?-1979 A)

Dove, The (La Paloma) (1859) w.m. Sebastian Yradier (1809-1865)

Down Among the Sheltering Palms (1914/15) w. James Brockman (1886/87-1967)
m. Abe Olman (1888-1984). (F) That Midnight Kiss, Some Like It Hot

Down By the Old Mill Stream (1910) w.m. Tell Taylor (1876-1937)

Down By the Riverside (Ain't gwine to study war no more) Traditional Black
American. (F) Colorado Sundown

Down in Honky Tonky Town (1916) w.m. Charles McCarron (1891-1919 A), Chris
Smith (1879-1949)

Doxology Old Hundred(th) (Praise God From Whom All Blessings Flow)
(1500's) w. Psalm 134 of the Genevan Psalter. m. Louis Bourgeois (1510?-15??)

Drink to Me Only with Thine Eyes (1780) w. Ben Jonson (1572-1637)
m. Anonymous

Drinking Song (Libiamo) (1853/54/55) From the opera "La Traviata." w. F.M. Piave
(1810-1876) m. G. Verdi (1813-1901)

Du und Du (1874) Waltz. From the operetta, "Die Fledermaus." m. Johann Strauss, Jr.
(1825-1899)

East Side, West Side (The Sidewalks of New York) (1894) w.m. Charles B.
Lawlor (1852-1925), James W. Blake (1862-1935). (F) Beau James

Easy Winners, The (1901) m. Scott Joplin (1868-1919)

Egmont Overture (1810) m. Ludwig van Beethoven (1770-1827)

1812 Overture (1882) m. Peter I. Tchaikovsky (1840-1893) (Op. 49). (F) Help!

Ein' Feste Burg see **Feste Burg, Ein'**

Eine Kleine Nachtmusik see **Kleine Nachtmusik, Eine**

El Capitan see **Capitan, El**

El Choclo see **Choclo, El**

Elijah (1846) w.m. Felix Mendelssohn (1809-1847)

Emperor Waltz (Kaiser-Walzer) (1889) m. Johann Strauss, Jr. (1825-1899)

Entertainer, The (1902) Piano Ragtime. m. Scott Joplin (1868-1919).
(F) The Sting. *The arrangement of this song done by Marvin Hamlisch
for the film, "The Sting," is* **not** *Public Domain.*

**Erie Canal (Fifteen Miles [Years] on the Erie Canal; Low Bridge! Everybody
Down)** (1913 for the Allen version) w.m. Thomas S. Allen or Traditional American.
*The version of this song by Thomas S. Allen or any version marked "Traditional" or
"Anonymous" is in the Public Domain.*

España (1884) Rhapsody for orchestra. m. Emmanuel Chabrier (1841-1894)

Estudiantina (1881/83) w. J. de Lau Lusignan m. Paul Lacome

Evening Prayer (1894) From the opera, "Hansel and Gretel." w. Adelheid Wette
(1858-1916) m. Engelbert Humperdinck (1854-1921). Also known as "Now I Lay Me
Down to Sleep."

Every Day is Ladies' Day with Me (1906) w. Henry Blossom (1866-1919)
m. Victor Herbert (1859-1924). (M) The Red Mill

Every Little Movement (Has a meaning all its own) (1910) w. Otto Harbach
(1873-1963) m. Karl Hoschna (1877-1911). (M) Madame Sherry (F) On Moonlight
Bay, The Jolson Story

Everybody's Doin' It Now (1911) w.m. Irving Berlin (1888-1989).
(M) Everybody's Doing it (F) Alexander's Ragtime Band, Easter Parade

Everything is Peaches Down in Georgia (1918) w. Grant Clarke (1891-1931)
m. Milton Ager (1893-1979), George W. Meyer (1884-1959). (M) U.S.

Faith of Our Fathers (1860's) w. Frederick Faber (1814-1863)
m. H.F. Hemy (1818-1888)

Fantaisie-Impromptu (1855) m. Frédéric Chopin (1810-1849) (Op. 66)

Farmer in the Dell, The Traditional American children's song

Fascination (1915) w.m. Harold R. Atteridge (1886-1938), Sigmund Romberg (1887-1951)

Feste Burg, Ein' (A Mighty Fortress Is Our God) (1500's) Traditional Protestant hymn. w.m. Martin Luther (1483-1546)

Fifteen Miles (Years) on the Erie Canal (Erie Canal; Low Bridge! Everybody Down) (1913 for the Allen version) w.m. Thomas S. Allen or Traditional American. *The version of this song by Thomas S. Allen or any version marked "Traditional" or "Anonymous" is in the Public Domain.*

Finlandia (1900) Symphonic poem. m. Jean Sibelius (1865-1957) (Op. 26)

First Noël, The (1883) Traditional Christmas carol

Fledermaus, Die (1874) Operetta. w. C. Haffner, R. Genée (1823-1895) m. Johann Strauss, Jr. (1825-1899)

Flight of the Bumblebee, The (1900) m. Nikolai Rimsky-Korsakov (1844-1908)

Flirtation Waltz (1889) m. John Talbot (1847-1905)

Flow Gently, Sweet Afton (1838) w. Robert Burns (1759-1796) m. Jonathan E. Spilman (1812-1896). (F) Pursuit to Algiers

Flying Trapeze, The (The Daring Young Man on the) (1868) w. George Leybourne (? -1884 P) m. Alfred Lee

For He's a Jolly Good Fellow (1700-1800's) Traditional English

For Me and My Gal (1917) w. Edgar Leslie (1885-1976) E. Ray Goetz (1886-1954) m. George W. Meyer (1884-1959). (M) Here and There (F) For Me and My Gal, Jolson Sings Again

Fort Sumpter March (1862) w. General Beauregard Wilks (1824-1875) m. Lionel Monk (1836-1880)

Forza del Destino, La (1862) Opera. w. F.M. Piave (1810-1876) m. Giuseppe Verdi (1813-1901)

Fountain in the Park, The (While Strolling Through the Park One Day) (1884) w.m. Ed Haley (1862/63-1932) (Ed Haley is a pseudonym of Robert A. King). (F) Hollywood Revue, Sunbonnet Sue

Four Seasons, The (1725) m. Antonio Vivaldi (1678-1741). (F) The Four Seasons

Frère Jacques (Are You Sleeping) (1800's) Traditional French children's song

From the Land of the Sky-Blue Water (1909) w. Nelle Richmond Eberhart (1871-1944) m. Charles Wakefield Cadman (1881-1946)

Funeral March (Marche Funèbre) (1840) From the Sonata in B-flat Minor for piano. m. Fréderic Chopin (1810-1849) (Op. 35)

Funeral March of a Marionette (1872) m. Charles Gounod (1818-1893)

Funiculì, Funiculà (1880) w. G. Turco m. Luigi Denza (1846-1922)

Für Elise (1810) m. Ludwig van Beethoven (1770-1827)

Gaudeamus Igitur (1781/82, based on a Latin manuscript dated 1287) Traditional student song. This German song is so old, the words are in Latin. Used by Johannes Brahms in the "Academic Festival Overture" (Op. 80).

Giannina Mia (1912) w. Otto Harbach (1873-1963) m. Rudolf Friml (1879-1972). (M) The Firefly (F) The Firefly

Girl I Left Behind Me, The (1810/18/55) w. Samuel Lover (1797-1868) m. Thomas Moore (1779-1852). Sung at West Point graduations. Words and music are based on traditional Irish and English materials. *There may also be versions that are Public Domain and are simply marked Traditional.*

Girl on the Magazine Cover (1915) w.m. Irving Berlin (1888-1989). (M) Stop! Look! Listen! (F) Easter Parade. *Sometimes called "Girl on the Magazine."*

Giselle (1841) Ballet. m. Adolph-Charles Adam (1803-1856)

Git Along Little Dogies (Whoopee ti yi yo) (Late 1800's) Traditional cowboy song. (F) Maisie

Give Me the Moonlight, Give Me the Girl (1917) w. Lew Brown (1893-1958) m. Albert von Tilzer (1878-1956). Theme song of Frankie Vaughan. (M) Hullo America (F) The Dolly Sisters

Give My Regards to Broadway (1904) w.m. George M. Cohan (1878-1942). (M) Little Johnny Jones, George M! (F) Little Johnny Jones, Yankee Doodle Dandy, Give My Regards to Broadway, Jolson Sings Again

Gladiator, The (1886) m. John Philip Sousa (1854-1932). *This song is associated with circuses.*

Gladiator's Entry, The (1900) m. Julius Fucik (1872-1916). This march is used to introduce circuses and wrestling matches around the world. (F) Heaven Can Wait

Glow-Worm, The (1902/07) w. English: Lilla Cayley Robinson w. German: Heinz Bolten-Bäckers m. Paul Lincke (1867-1946). (M) The Girl Behind the Counter. *In 1952, Johnny Mercer added new lyrics to this music. His new lyrics are considered the standard American version. The Mercer lyric is* **not** *Public Domain.*

Go Down Moses Traditional Black American. *Henry (aka Harry) Thacker (H.T.) Burleigh (1866/86-1949) did arrangements of many traditional spirituals and popularized them in the early decades of the 1900's. The arrangement of this song done by H.T. Burleigh is in the Public Domain.*

God Rest Ye Merry Gentlemen Traditional Christmas carol

God Save the King (1700's) Traditional English

Gold and Silver Waltz (1903/04) m. Franz Lehar (1870-1948) (Op. 75)

Goldberg Variations (1742) m. J. S. Bach (1685-1750)

Golden Slippers (Oh Dem Golden Slippers) (1879) w.m. James A. Bland (1854-1911). (F) Tulsa Kid

Golliwogg's Cake Walk (1908) From "The Children's Corner" for piano. m. Claude Debussy (1862-1918)

Good Christian Men, Rejoice Traditional Christmas carol. w. Rev. John Mason Neale (1818-1866) m. Anonymous

Good King Wenceslas Traditional Christmas carol. w. Rev. John Mason Neale (1818-1866) m. Anonymous

Good Man is Hard to Find, A (1918) w.m. Eddie Green (1901-1950) (M) Back Again, Me and Bessie (F) Meet Danny Wilson

Good Night Ladies (1847/53) w.m. E. P. Christy (1815-1862)

Good-Bye Broadway, Hello, France! (1917) w. C. Francis Reisner (1887-1962 A), Benny Davis (1895-1979) m. Billy Baskette (1884-1949 A). World War I song. (M) The Passing Show of 1917

Goodbye, Girls, I'm Through (1914) w. John L. Golden (1874-1955) m. Ivan Caryll (1860/61-1921). (M) Chin-Chin

Goodbye, Good Luck, God Bless You (1916) w. J. Keirn Brennan (1873-1948) m. Ernest R. Ball (1878-1927)

Goodbye, My Lady Love (1904) w.m. Joseph E. Howard (1878-1961)

Götterdämmerung (1873/74) Opera. w.m. Richard Wagner (1813-1883). One of four operas that comprise Der Ring des Nibelungen.

Grandfather's Clock (1876) w.m. Henry Clay Work (1832-1884)

Greensleeves (1580) Traditional English

Gypsy Love Song (Slumber on) (1898) w. Harry B. Smith (1860-1936) m. Victor Herbert (1859-1924). (M) The Fortune Teller (F) Love Happy

Habanera (1875) From the opera, "Carmen." w. H. Meilhac (1831-1897), L. Halévy (1834-1908) m. Georges Bizet (1838-1875)

Hail, Hail, the Gang's All Here, What the H-- Do We Care (1917) w. D.A. Esrom (1890-1953) (D.A. Esrom is one of the pseudonyms for Theodora Morse) m. Theodore F. Morse (1873/74-1924), based on "Come, Friends, Who Plough the Sea" from "The Pirates of Penzance" (Gilbert & Sullivan)

Hail to the Chief (1812/14) March. w. Sir Walter Scott, (1771-1832) m. (?) James Sanderson (1769-1841). *This march is traditionally played to announce the arrival of the President of the United States.*

Hallelujah Chorus (1767/ published after Handel's death) From the oratorio, "Messiah." w. compiled and adapted from the Bible by Charles Jennens (1700-1773) m. George Frederick Handel (1685-1759)

Hand Me Down My Walking Cane (1880?) w.m. James A. Bland (1854-1911)

Hands Across the Sea (1899) March. m. John Philip Sousa (1854-1932)

Happy Farmer, The (The Merry Peasant) (1849) m. Robert Schumann (1810-1856) (Op. 68). *This song was used as a recurring theme in the film, "The Wizard of Oz."*

Hark! The Herald Angels Sing (1855) Traditional Christmas carol. w. Charles Wesley (1707-1788) m. Felix Mendelssohn (1809-1847)

Harrigan (1907) w.m. George M. Cohan (1878-1942). (M) Fifty Miles from Boston, George M! (F) Yankee Doodle Dandy

Has Anybody Here Seen Kelly? (1910) w.m. C.W. Murphy (? -1913 P), Will Letters (? -1938 P), John Charles Moore (?-1938 P), William J. McKenna (1881-1950). *Note: PRS says that Will Letters and John Moore are the same person.* (M) The Jolly Bachelors

Have a Heart (1916) w. P.G. Wodehouse (1881-1975) or Gene Buck (1885-1957) m. Jerome Kern (1885-1945). (M) Have a Heart. *Wodehouse and Kern are credited for the song from the musical, "Have a Heart."*

He is an Englishman (1878) From the operetta, "H.M.S. Pinafore." w. W.S. Gilbert (1836-1911) m. Arthur Sullivan (1842-1900)

Hearts and Flowers (1899) w. Mary D. Brine (1836-1925) m. Theodore Moses Tobani (1855-1933). Used in the silent movie era for scenes where the villain is demanding payment of the mortgage "or else."

Hello, Frisco, Hello (1915) w. Gene Buck (1885-1957) m. Louis A. Hirsch (1887-1924). (M) Ziegfeld Follies of 1915 (F) Wharf Angel

Hello, Ma Baby (1899) w.m. Joseph E. Howard (1878-1961), Ida Emerson

Here We Go/Come A-Caroling/A-Wassailing (Wassail Song) Traditional Christmas carol

He's a Devil in His Own Home Town (1914) w. Grant Clarke (1891-1931), Irving Berlin (1888-1989) m. Irving Berlin (1888-1989)

Hey, Diddle Diddle Traditional Mother Goose children's song

Hickory Dickory Dock Traditional Mother Goose children's song

Hindustan (1918) w.m. Oliver G. Wallace (1887-1963 A), Harold Weeks (1893-1967 A). (M) Joy Bells

Hold That Tiger! (Tiger Rag) (1917) m. The Original Dixieland Jazz Band. (F) Is Everybody Happy, The Big Broadcast, Birth of the Blues, Has Anybody Seen My Gal, Night Club Girl. *Only the instrumental version of this selection is in the Public Domain. There are words to this song by Harry DeCosta. The DeCosta words are* **not** *Public Domain. The version that is in the Public Domain is the one by The Original Dixieland Jazz Band.*

Holly and the Ivy, The Traditional Christmas carol

Holy, Holy, Holy, Lord God Almighty (1861) w. Reginald Heber (1783-1826) m. John Bacchus Dykes (1823-1876)

Home on the Range (Oh, give me a home where the buffalo roam) (1873 words/1905 music) w. Brewster Higley (1823-1911) m. Daniel Kelley. (F) The Fighting Coast Guard

Home Sweet Home (Be it ever so humble) (1823) w. John Howard Payne (1791-1852) m. Henry Bishop (1786-1855)

Hootchy Kootchy Dance (Streets of Cairo, The) (Oh they don't wear pants in the southern part of France) (1893/95) w.m. James Thornton (1861-1938)

Hot Cross Buns Traditional Mother Goose children's song

Hot Time in the Old Town Tonight (There'll Be a) (1896) w. Joseph Hayden (? - 1937) m. Theodore A. Metz (1848-1936). (M) Me and Bessie

How You ('Ya) Going to Keep 'Em Down on the Farm After They've Seen Paree? (1919) w. Sam M. Lewis (1885-1959), Joe Young (1889-1939) m. Walter Donaldson (1893-1947). (F) For Me and My Gal, The Eddie Cantor Story

How'd You Like to Spoon with Me? (1915) w. Edward Laska (1884-1959 A) m. Jerome Kern (1885-1945). (M) The Earl and the Girl (F) Till the Clouds Roll By

How's Every Little Thing in Dixie (1916) w. Jack Yellen (1892-1991 A) m. Albert Gumble (1883-1946 A)

Humoresque (1894) m. Antonin Dvorák (1841-1904) (Op.101, No. 7)

Humpty Dumpty Traditional Mother Goose children's song

Hungarian Dance No. 5 (1859/69) m. Johannes Brahms (1833-1897), based on a theme by Kéler.

Hungarian Rhapsody No. 2 (1851) m. Franz Liszt (1811-1886)

I Ain't Got Nobody (1916) w. Roger Graham (1885-1938) m. Spencer Williams (1889-1965), Dave Peyton. Theme song of Bert Williams. (F) Paris Honeymoon

I Am the Yankee Doodle Boy (1904) w.m. George M. Cohan (1878-1942). (M) Little Johnny Jones, George M!, Dancin' (F) Little Johnny Jones, Yankee Doodle Dandy, The Seven Little Foys

I Didn't Raise My Boy to Be a Soldier (1915) w. Alfred Bryan (1871-1958 A) m. Al Piantadosi (1884-1955)

I Don't Care (1905) w. Jean Lenox m. Harry O. Sutton. Theme song of Eva Tanguay. (F) In the Good Old Summertime

I Don't Want to Play in Your Yard (1894) w. Phillip Wingate m. Henry W. Petrie (1857-1925)

I Heard the Bells on Christmas Day Traditional Christmas carol. w. H.W. Longfellow (1807-1882) (adapted) m. John Baptiste Calkin (1827-1905)

I Love a Lassie (Ma Scotch Bluebell) (1906/07) w.m. Harry Lauder (1870-1950), Gerald Grafton. Theme song of Harry Lauder.

I Love a Piano (1915) w.m. Irving Berlin (1888-1989). (M) Follow the Crowd, Stop! Look! Listen! (F) Easter Parade

I Love You So (The Merry Widow Waltz) (1905/07) w. Adrian Ross (1859-1933) m. Franz Lehar (1870-1948). (M) The Merry Widow (F) The Merry Widow

I Love You Truly (1901) w.m. Carrie Jacobs-Bond (1862-1946)

I Might Be Your Once-In-A-While (1919) w. Robert B. Smith (1875-1951) m. Victor Herbert (1859-1924). (M) Angel Face (F) The Great Victor Herbert

I Saw Three Ships Traditional Christmas carol

I Used to Love You, But It's All Over Now (1920) w. Lew Brown (1893-1958), m. Albert Von Tilzer (1878-1956)

I Want a Girl (Just Like the Girl That Married Dear Old Dad) (1911) w. William A. Dillon (1877-1966) m. Harry von Tilzer (1872-1946). (F) Show Business, The Jolson Story

I Want to Go Back to Michigan, Down on the Farm (1914) w.m. Irving Berlin (1888-1989). (M) 5064 Gerard (F) Easter Parade

I Wish I Could Shimmy (Shemmi) Like My Sister Kate (1919) w.m. Armand J. Piron (1888-1943 A). *Pre-flapper dance.*

I Wish I Had a Girl (1907/08) w. Gus Kahn (1886-1941) m. Grace LeBoy Kahn (1891-1983 A). (F) I'll See You in My Dreams

I Wonder Who's Kissing Her Now (1909) w. Will M. Hough (1882-1962), Frank R. Adams (1883/84-1963) m. Joseph E. Howard (1878-1961), Harold Orlob (1883/85-1982 A). (M) The Prince of Tonight (F) The Time the Place and the Girl, I Wonder Who's Kissing Her Now

I'd Love to Live in Loveland (With a girl like you) (1910) w.m. W.R. Williams (1867-1954 A)

Ida, Sweet as Apple Cider (1903) w. Eddie Leonard (1875-1941 A) m. Eddie Munson. (F) Babes in Arms, Incendiary Blonde, The Eddie Cantor Story

If I Had My Way (1913) w. Lou Klein (1888-1945 A) m. James Kendis (1883-1946 A). (F) If I Had My Way, Sunbonnet Sue

If I Were on the Stage (Kiss Me Again) (1905) w. Henry Blossom (1866-1919) m. Victor Herbert (1859-1924). (M) Mlle. Modiste (F) The Great Victor Herbert

If You Don't Want My Peaches, You'd Better Stop Shaking My Tree (1914) w.m. Irving Berlin (1888-1989)

If You Had All the World and Its Gold (1916) w.m. Bartley Costello (1871-1941), Harry Edelheit (1891-1955 A), Al Piantadosi (1884-1955)

If You Were the Only Girl in the World (1916) w. Clifford Grey (1887-1941) m. Nat D. Ayer (1887-1952). (M) The Bing Boys Are Here (F) The Vagabond Lover, Both Ends of the Candle. *Many arrangements and a "new edition" of this song were created in the year 1925. The arrangements and the "new edition" are **not** Public Domain. You need to use the song as it was published in 1916.*

I'll Be With You in Apple Blossom Time (1920) w. Neville Fleeson (1887-1945 A) m. Albert von Tilzer (1878-1956). (F) Buck Privates

I'll Build a Stairway to Paradise (1922) w. Bud (B.G.) De Sylva (1895-1950), Arthur Francis (1896-1983) (Arthur Francis is a pseudonym of Ira Gershwin) m. George Gershwin (1898-1937). (M) George White's Scandals of 1922, Stop Flirting (F) Rhapsody in Blue, An American in Paris

I'll Take You Home Again, Kathleen (1876) w.m. Thomas P. Westendorf (1848-1923)

Il Est Né, Le Devin Enfant (1800's) Traditional French Christmas Carol. *There seem to be many English translations, written at different times. If you are using an English translation, make sure it is in the Public Domain. You can check with BZ/Rights Stuff about this.*

I'm All Bound 'Round with the Mason-Dixon Line (1917) w. Sam M. Lewis (1885-1959), Joe Young (1889-1939) m. Jean Schwartz (1878-1956)

I'm Always Chasing Rainbows (1918) w. Joseph McCarthy (1885-1943) m. Harry Carroll (1892-1962). (M) Oh, Look!, Ziegfeld Girl (F) The Dolly Sisters, The Merry Monahans

I'm Called Little Buttercup (1878) From the operetta, "H.M.S. Pinafore." w. W.S. Gilbert (1836-1911) m. Arthur Sullivan (1842-1900)

I'm Falling in Love with Someone (1910) w. Rida Johnson Young (1869-1926) m. Victor Herbert (1859-1924). (M) Naughty Marietta (F) Naughty Marietta,The Great Victor Herbert

I'm Forever Blowing Bubbles (1919) w.m. Jaan/Jean Kenbrovin, John William Kellette. Jaan/Jean Kenbrovin is a pseudonym for Nathaniel H. Vincent (1889/90-1979 A). John William Kellette is a pseudonym for James Brockman (1886/87-1967) and James Kendis (1883-1946 A) and may also be a pseudonym for Nathaniel H. Vincent (1889/90-1979 A). Available records are somewhat confusing as to whether Kellette is a pseudonym for Vincent. (M) The Passing Show of 1918 (F) On Moonlight Bay

I'm Just Wild About Harry (1921) w.m. Noble Sissle (1889-1975 A), Eubie Blake (1883-1983 A). (M) Shuffle Along, Eubie! (F) Babes in Arms, Rose of Washington Square, Broadway, Is Everybody Happy, Jolson Sings Again

I'm Nobody's Baby (1921) w.m. Benny Davis (1895-1979), Milton Ager (1893-1979), Lester Santly (1895-1983). Arrangement by Milton Ager. The arrangement of this song by Milton Ager is in the Public Domain. (F) Andy Hardy Meets a Debutante

I'm Sorry I Made You Cry (1916) w.m. N.J. Clesi. (F) Somebody Loves Me, Rose of Washington Square

In a Monastery Garden (1915) m. Albert William Ketelbey (1875-1959)

In My Merry Oldsmobile (1905) w. Vincent P. Bryan (1883-1937) m. Gus Edwards (1879-1945). (M) The Merry Monahans

(In My Sweet Little) Alice Blue Gown (1919) w. Joseph McCarthy (1885-1943) m. Harry Tierney (1890-1965). (M) Irene (F) Irene

In Old New York (The Streets of New York) (1906) w. Henry Blossom (1866-1919) m. Victor Herbert (1859-1924). (M) The Red Mill

In the Evening by the Moonlight (1879) w.m. James A. Bland (1854-1911)

In the Garden (1912) w.m. C. Austin Miles (1868-1946). *This song is famous for its chorus "and He walks with me, and He talks with me."*

In the Gloaming (1877) w. Meta Orred m. Annie Fortescue Harrison (1851-1944)

In the Good Old Summertime (1902) w. Ren Shields (1868-1913) m. George Evans (1870-1915). (M) The Defender (F) In the Good Old Summertime

In the Great Somewhere (1919) Traditional Black American. *Henry (aka Harry) Thacker (H.T.) Burleigh (1866/86-1949) did arrangements of many traditional spirituals and popularized them in the early decades of the 1900's. The arrangement of this song by H.T. Burleigh is in the Public Domain.*

In the Hall of the Mountain King (1874/75) m. Edvard Grieg (1843-1907)

In the Shade of the Old Apple Tree (1905) w. Harry H. Williams (1879-1922) m. Egbert van Alstyne (1882-1951)

In the Sweet Bye and Bye (1902) w. Vincent P. Bryan (1883-1937) m. Harry von Tilzer (1872-1946)

Indiana (Back Home Again in) (1917) w. Ballard MacDonald (1882-1935 A) m. James F. Hanley (1892-1942 A). (F) With a Song in My Heart, Satchmo the Great, Drum Crazy, The Five Pennies

Indianola (1917) m. S.R. Henry, D. Onivas (1882-1973) (D. Onivas is a pseudonym of Domenico Savino). *Only the instrumental music of this selection is in the Public Domain.*

Ireland is Ireland to Me (1915) w. Fiske O'Hara (1878-1945), J. Keirn Brennan (1873-1948) m. Ernest R. Ball (1878-1927)

Ireland Must Be Heaven, for My Mother Came from There (1916) w.m. Joseph McCarthy (1885-1943), Howard Johnson (1887-1941 A), Fred Fisher (1875-1942), **or** w. Joseph McCarthy (1885-1943), Howard Johnson (1887-1941 A) m. (and arrangement) Fred Fisher (1875-1942). (F) Oh You Beautiful Doll

Irish Washerwoman, The (1792) Traditional Irish dance tune

It Came Upon a Midnight Clear (1849/50) Traditional Christmas carol. w. Edmund H. Sears (1810-1876) m. Richard Storrs Willis (1819-1900)

Italian Street Song (1910) w. Rida Johnson Young (1869-1926) m. Victor Herbert (1859-1924). (M) Naughty Marietta (F) Naughty Marietta

It's a Long, Long Way to Tipperary (1912) w.m. Jack Judge (1878-1938), Harry Williams. World War I song. (M) Chin-Chin, Dancing Around (F) Wait Till the Sun Shines Nellie, What Price Glory?

It's Delightful to Be Married (1906/07) w. Anna Held (1873?-1918) m. Vincent Scotto (1876-1952). (F) The Parisian Model

It's Tulip Time in Holland (1915) w. Dave Radford (1884-1968 A) m. Richard A. Whiting (1891-1938). (F) April Showers

I've Been Working on the Railroad (Someone's in the kitchen with Dinah) (1894) Traditional American

I've Got Rings on My Fingers (1909/10) w. R.P. Weston (1878-1936), F.J. Barnes m. Maurice Scott (?-1933 P) (M) The Midnight Sons, The Yankee Girl

I've Got the Time—I've Got the Place, but It's Hard to Find the Girl (1910) w. Ballard MacDonald (1882-1935 A) m. S.R. Henry

Ja-Da, Ja-Da, Ja-Da Jing-Jing-Jing (1918) w.m. Bob Carleton (1896-1956 A). (M) Bran Pie

Jack and Jill Traditional Mother Goose children's song

Jack Be Nimble Traditional Mother Goose children's song

Jack Sprat Traditional Mother Goose children's song

Japanese Sandman, The (1920) w. Raymond B. Egan (1890-1952) m. Richard A. Whiting (1891-1938)

Jarabe Tapatio (Mexican Hat Dance) (1919) m. F.A. Partichela

Jazz Me Blues (1920/21) w.m. Tom Delaney

Jeannie with the Light Brown Hair (1854) w.m. Stephen Foster (1826-1864). (F) Swanee River, I Dream Of Jeannie

Jelly Roll Blues (1915) w.m. Ferdinand "Jelly Roll" Morton (1885/90-1941).
  (M) Jelly's Last Jam

Jesu, Joy of Man's Desiring (1723) Chorale prelude. m. J.S. Bach (1685-1750)

Jimmy Crack Corn (The Blue Tail Fly) (1846) Traditional American

Jingle Bells (1857) Traditional Christmas carol. w.m. J. Pierpont (1822-1893)
  (M) The 1940's Radio Hour

Joe Turner Blues (1915/16) w.m. W.C. Handy (1873-1958)

John Brown's Body (1861) w. Anonymous m. Same as "The Battle Hymn of
  the Republic"

Johnny Get Your Gun (1886) w.m. Monroe Rosenfeld (1861/62-1918)

Jolly Old St. Nicholas Traditional Christmas carol

Joshua Fit de Battle of Jericho Traditional Black American

Joy to the World (1839) Traditional Christmas carol. w. Isaac Watts (1674-1748)
  m. Lowell Mason (1792-1872)

Jupiter Symphony (1793/ published after Mozart's death) Symphony No. 41.
  m. W.A. Mozart (1756-1791)

Just a Song at Twilight (Love's Old Sweet Song) (1884) w. C. Clifton Bingham
  (1859-1913) m. J.L. Molloy (1837-1909). (F) Wait Till the Sun Shines Nellie

Just A-Wearyin' for You (1901) w. Frank L. Stanton (1857-1927) m. Carrie Jacobs-
  Bond (1862-1946)

Kaiser-Walzer (Emperor Waltz) (1889) m. Johann Strauss, Jr. (1825-1899)

Katinka (1916) w. Otto Harbach (1873-1963) m. Rudolf Friml (1879-1972).
(M) Katinka. *There is another song called "Katinka," written by Russell and Tobias in 1926. The Russell and Tobias song is **not** Public Domain.*

Keep the Home-Fires Burning (Till the boys come home) (1914/15)
w. Lena Guilbert Ford m. Ivor Novello (1893-1951). World War I song

Kentucky Babe (Sleep, Kentucky babe) (1896) w. Richard Henry Buck (1870-1956 A) m. Adam Geibel (1855-1933)

Kerry Dance (O the days of the Kerry dancing) (1870's) w.m. J.L. Molloy (1837-1909)

King Cotton (1895) March. m. John Philip Sousa (1854-1932)

Kiss in the Dark, A (1922) w. Bud (B.G.) De Sylva (1895-1950) m. Victor Herbert (1859-1924). (M) Orange Blossoms (F) The Great Victor Herbert, Look for the Silver Lining

Kiss Me Again (If I Were on the Stage) (1905) w. Henry Blossom (1866-1919) m. Victor Herbert (1859-1924). (M) Mlle. Modiste (F) The Great Victor Herbert

Kitten on the Keys (1921) m. Edward E. (Zez) Confrey (1895-1971). Piano solo.

K-K-K-Katy (1918) w.m. Geoffrey O'Hara (1882-1967). (M) Buzz, The Glorious Days (F) The Cockeyed World, Tin Pan Alley

Kleine Nachtmusik, Eine (1787/1827) Serenade for strings. m. W.A. Mozart (1756-1791)

L'Amour-Toujours-L'Amour (Love Everlasting) (1922) w. Catherine Chisholm Cushing (1874-1952) m. Rudolf Friml (1879-1972)

Largo (1894) From "The New World Symphony." m. Antonin Dvorák (1841-1904). *This melody was used for a song called "Goin' Home" (words by William Fisher). "Goin' Home" is **not** Public Domain. What is Public Domain is the "Largo" as Dvorák wrote it.*

Last Days of Pompeii, The (1912) m. John Philip Sousa (1854-1932)

Lead, Kindly Light (1868) w. John Henry Newman m. John Bacchus Dykes (1823-1876)

Leonore Overture No. 3 (1806/10) m. Ludwig van Beethoven (1770-1827)

Let Me Call You Sweetheart (1910) w.m. Beth Slater Whitson (1879-1930), Leo Friedman (1869-1927 A)

Let the Rest of the World Go By (1919) w. J. Keirn Brennan (1873-1948) m. Ernest R. Ball (1878-1927)

Let Us Break Bread Together Traditional Black American

Liebesfreud (1910) m. Fritz Kreisler (1875-1962)

Liebesleid (1910) m. Fritz Kreisler (1875-1962)

Liebestod (1859/60) From the opera, "Tristan und Isolde." w.m. Richard Wagner (1813-1883)

Liebestraum (1847) m. Franz Liszt (1811-1886)

Lift Every Voice and Sing (1900/10) w.m. James Weldon Johnson (1871-1938), J. Rosamond Johnson (1873-1954)

Light Cavalry Overture (1868) m. Franz von Suppé (1819-1895)

Li'l Liza Jane (1916) w.m. Countess Ada Goudard de Lachau (?-1956)

Lily of the Valley (1917) w. L. Wolfe Gilbert (1886-1970) m. Anatole Friedland (1881-1938 A)

Limehouse Blues (1922) w. Douglas Furber (1885/86-1961) m. Philip Braham (?-1934 P), arrangement by Philip Braham (?-1934 P). (M) A to Z, Andre Charlot's Revue of 1924 (F) Ziegfeld Follies. *The 1922 arrangement by Philip Braham is in the Public Domain in the United States.*

Listen to the Mocking Bird (1855) w. Alice Hawthorne (1827-1902) (Alice Hawthorne is a pseudonym of Septimus Winner) m. Richard Milburn

Little Annie Rooney (1889/90) w.m. Michael Nolan

Little Bit of Heaven, Sure They Call It Ireland, A (1914) w. J. Keirn Brennan (1873-1948) m. Ernest R. Ball (1878-1927). (M) The Heart of Paddy Whack (F) A Little Bit of Heaven, My Wild Irish Rose

Little Bo-Peep Traditional Mother Goose children's song

Little Boy Blue Traditional Mother Goose children's song

Little Brown Jug (1869) w.m. Joseph E. Winner (1837-1918). (M) The 1940's Radio Hour (F) Hired Wife

Little David Play on Your Harp (1921) Traditional Black American. *Henry (aka Harry) Thacker (H.T.) Burleigh (1866/86-1949) did arrangements of many traditional spirituals and popularized them in the early decades of the 1900's. The arrangement of this song by H.T. Burleigh is in the Public Domain.*

Little Grey Home in the West (1911) w. D. Eardley-Wilmot m. Hermann Lohr (1871-1943)

Little Jack Horner Traditional Mother Goose children's song

Little Love, a Little Kiss, A (1911/12) w. French: Nilson Fysher (? -1931 P) w. English: Adrian Ross (1859-1933) m. Lao Silesu (? -1953 P). (M) Ziegfeld Follies of 1913

Little Miss Muffet Traditional Mother Goose children's song

Little Mother of Mine (1917) w. Walter H. Brown m. Henry T. Burleigh (1866/86-1949)

Little Sir Echo (1917) w. Laura Rountree Smith (1876-1924) m. John S. Fearis (1867-1932). *There is another song by the same title, with words and music by Joe Marsala and Adele Girard that is* **not** *Public Domain.*

Little Tommy Tucker Traditional Mother Goose children's song

Loads of Lovely Love (1903) w. Jeanne Wilson (1865-1938) m. Henry Chalfont (1882-1953)

Loch Lomond (Oh! ye'll take the high road) (1800's) Traditional Scottish. (F) Pursuit to Algiers

London Bridge Traditional English

Londonderry Air (1855) Traditional Irish. *The song, "Danny Boy," was based on this song. "Danny Boy" is* **also** *Public Domain.*

Long, Long Ago (1830/40's) w.m. Thomas Haynes Bayly (1797-1839). (F) Calling Wild Bill Elliott

Look for the Silver Lining (1920) w. Bud (B.G.) De Sylva (1895-1950) m. Jerome Kern (1885-1945). (M) Sally (F) Meet Me in St. Louis, Look for the Silver Lining

Lost Chord, The (1877) w. Adelaide A. Proctor (1825-1864) m. Arthur Sullivan (1842-1900)

Love is the Best of All (1915) w. Henry Blossom (1866-1919) m. Victor Herbert (1859-1924). (M) The Princess Pat

Love Me and the World is Mine (1906) w. Dave Reed, Jr. (1872/73-1946) m. Ernest R. Ball (1878-1927)

Love Nest, The (1920) w. Otto Harbach (1873-1963) m. Louis A. Hirsch (1887-1924). Theme song of Burns and Allen radio and television programs. (M) Mary (F) Both Ends of the Candle

Love's Old Sweet Song (Just a Song at Twilight) (1884) w. C. Clifton Bingham (1859-1913) m. J.L. Molloy (1837-1909). (F) Wait Till the Sun Shines Nellie

(I've Got the) Lovesick Blues (1922) w. Irving Mills (1894-1985) m. Cliff Friend (1893-1974)

Low Bridge! Everybody Down (Erie Canal; Fifteen Miles [Years] on the Erie Canal) (1913 for the Allen version) w.m. Thomas S. Allen or Traditional American. *The version of this song by Thomas S. Allen or any version marked "Traditional" or "Anonymous" is in the Public Domain.*

Lullaby (Wiegenlied) (1868) m. Johannes Brahms (1833-1897) (Op. 49)

Lully, Lullay (The Coventry Carol) Traditional Christmas carol

Ma! He's Making Eyes at Me (1921) w. Sidney Clare (1892-1972 A) m. Con Conrad (1891-1938) (Con Conrad is a pseudonym of Conrad K. Dober). (M) The Midnight Rounders (F) Ma, He's Making Eyes at Me

MacNamara's Band (1917) w. John J. Stamford m. Shamus O'Connor. (F) I'll Get By, Bad Lands of Dakota

Madama Butterfly (1904) Opera. w. Luigi Illica (1857-1919), Giuseppe Giacosa (1847-1906) m. Giacomo Puccini (1858-1924)

Magic Flute, The (Die Zauberflöte) (1791) Opera. w. E. Schikaneder (1751-1812) m. W.A. Mozart (1756-1791)

Mammy O' Mine (1919) w. William Tracey (1893-1957 A) m. Maceo Pinkard (1897-1962)

Man On the Flying Trapeze, The (The Daring Young Man) (1868) w. George Leybourne (? -1884 P) m. Alfred Lee

Mandy (1919) w.m. Irving Berlin (1888-1989). (M) Yip! Yip! Yaphank, The Ziegfeld Follies of 1919, This Is the Army. (F) Kid Millions, White Christmas

Manhattan Beach March (1893) m. John Philip Sousa (1854-1932)

Maple Leaf Rag (1899) m. Scott Joplin (1868-1919)

March (1845/46) From the opera, "Tannhaüser." m. Richard Wagner (1813-1883)

March of the Dwarfs (1891) m. Edvard Grieg (1843-1907) (Op. 54)

March of the Toys (1903) m. Victor Herbert (1859-1924). (M) Babes in Toyland (F) Babes in Toyland, The Great Victor Herbert

Marche du Sacre, La (Coronation March) (1849) From the opera, "Le Prophète." m. Giacomo Meyerbeer (1791-1864)

Marche Funèbre (Funeral March) (1840) From the Sonata in B-flat Minor for piano. m. Fréderic Chopin (1810-1849) (Op. 35)

Marche Slave (1879) m. Peter I. Tchaikovsky (1840-1893) (Op. 31)

Marching Through Georgia (1865) Civil War song. w.m. Henry Clay Work (1832-1884)

Margie (1920) w. Benny Davis (1895-1979) m. Con Conrad (1891-1938) (Con Conrad is a pseudonym of Conrad K. Dober), J. Russell Robinson (1892-1963). (F) Margie, The Eddie Cantor Story

Marines' Hymn (From the halls of Montezuma) (m. 1868 w. 1917/19) m. Jacques Offenbach (1819-1880) *The music for this song comes from "Geneviève de Brabant," an opéra bouffe by Offenbach. The words were written much later and who wrote them is uncertain.*

Marseillaise, La (1792) French National Anthem. w.m. Claude Rouget de Lisle (1760-1836)

Mary Had a Little Lamb (1867/68) w. Sarah Josepha Hale (1788-1879) m. E.P. Christy (1815-1862) (Same as the second part of "Good Night Ladies")

Maryland, My Maryland (1861) w. James Ryder Randall (1839-1908) m. Same as "O Tännenbaum, O Tännenbaum"

Mary's a Grand Old Name (1905) w.m. George M. Cohan (1878-1942). (M) Forty-Five Minutes From Broadway (F) Yankee Doodle Dandy, The Seven Little Foys

Massa's in de Cold (Cold) Ground (1852) w.m. Stephen Foster (1826-1864)

Meet Me in St. Louis, Louis (1904) w. Andrew B. Sterling (1874-1955) m. Kerry Mills (1869-1948). (F) Meet Me in St. Louis

Meet Me Tonight in Dreamland (1909) w. Beth Slater Whitson (1879-1930) m. Leo Friedman (1869-1927 A). (F) In the Good Old Summertime

Melody in F (1850's) m. Anton Rubinstein (1829/30-1894) (Op. 3)

Memories (1915) w. Gus Kahn (1886-1941) m. Egbert van Alstyne (1882-1951). (F) I'll See You in My Dreams

Memphis Blues, The (1913) w. George A. Norton (1880-1923) m. W.C. Handy (1873-1958). (F) Birth of the Blues, St. Louis Blues

Mer, La (1903/05) From "Symphonic Sketches." m. Claude Debussy (1862-1918)

Merry Peasant, The (The Happy Farmer) (1849) m. Robert Schumann (1810-1856) (Op. 68). *This song was used as a recurring theme in the film, "The Wizard of Oz."*

Merry Widow Waltz, The (I Love You So) (1905/07) w. Adrian Ross (1859-1933) m. Franz Lehar (1870-1948). (M) The Merry Widow (F) The Merry Widow

Messiah (1767/ published after Handel's death) Oratorio. w. Compiled and adapted from the Bible by Charles Jennens (1700-1773) m. George Frederick Handel (1685-1759). This work contains the famous "Hallelujah Chorus."

Mexican Hat Dance (Jarabe Tapatio) (1919) m. F.A. Partichela

Mighty Fortress is Our God, A (Ein' Feste Burg) (1500's) Traditional Protestant hymn. w.m. Martin Luther (1483-1546)

Mighty Lak' a Rose (1901) w. Frank L. Stanton (1857-1927) m. Ethelbert Nevin (1862-1901)

Minuet in G (1796) m. Ludwig van Beethoven (1770-1827)

Minuet in G (1887) m. Ignace Paderewski (1860-1941) (Op.14)

Minute Waltz (1846/47) m. Fréderic Chopin (1810-1849) (Op. 64, No. 1)

M-I-S-S-I-S-S-I-P-P-I (1916) w. Bert Hanlon (1890-1972 A), Ben Ryan (1887/92-1968 A) m. Harry Tierney (1890-1965). (M) Hitchy-Koo, The Beauty Spot

Missouri Waltz, The (Hush-a-bye, ma baby) (1914) Official State Song of Missouri. w. James Royce Shannon (1881-1946 A) m. Frederick Knight Logan (1871-1928), based on an original melody by John V. Eppell

Mister Gallagher and Mister Shean (1922) w.m. Ed Gallagher, Al Shean (1868-1949). (M) Ziegfeld Follies of 1922 (F) Ziegfeld Girl. *The U.S. Copyright Office shows a renewal of this song by Edward Gallagher, Jr., as child of the author in 1949. This information could lead to the presumption that Edward Gallagher was dead by 1949. Consult your attorney. We have no other reliable information on Gallagher's birth and death dates.*

Mistress Mary Quite Contrary Traditional Mother Goose children's song

Modern Major General (1879/80) From the operetta "The Pirates of Penzance." w. W.S. Gilbert (1836-1911) m. Arthur Sullivan (1842-1900)

Molly Malone [Sweet] (Cockles and Mussels) Traditional Irish

Moonbeams (1906) w. Henry Blossom (1866-1919) m. Victor Herbert (1859-1924). (M) The Red Mill

Moonlight Bay (On Moonlight Bay) (1912) w. Edward Madden (1877-1952) m. Percy Wenrich (1880/87-1952). (F) On Moonlight Bay, Tin Pan Alley

Moonlight Sonata (1802) m. Ludwig van Beethoven (1770-1827). Famous first movement (Op. 27, No. 2)

M-O-T-H-E-R (A Word That Means the World to Me) (1915) w. Howard Johnson (1887-1941 A) m. Theodore F. Morse (1873/74-1924)

Mother Machree (1910) w. Rida Johnson Young (1869-1926) m. Chauncey Olcott (1858-1932), Ernest R. Ball (1878-1927). (M) Barry of Ballymore (F) My Wild Irish Rose

Mulberry Bush Traditional Mother Goose children's song

Musetta's Waltz (1896) From the opera, "La Bohème." w. Giuseppe Giacosa (1847-1906), Luigi Illica (1857-1919) m. Giacomo Puccini (1858-1924)

My Best Girl's a New Yorker (Corker) (1895) w.m. John Stromberg (1853-1902)

My Bonnie Lies Over the Ocean (1881) Traditional

My Buddy (1922) w. Gus Kahn (1886-1941) m. Walter Donaldson (1893-1947). (F) I'll See You in My Dreams

My Gal Sal (1905) w.m. Paul Dresser (1857-1906). (F) My Gal Sal

My Heart at Thy Sweet Voice (1876) From the opera, "Samson and Delilah." w. F. Lemaire m. Camille Saint-Saëns (1835-1921)

My Hero (1909) w. Stanislaus Stange (?-1917) m. Oscar Straus (1870-1954). (M) The Chocolate Soldier (F) The Chocolate Soldier, Two Weeks With Love

My Little Girl (1915) w. Sam M. Lewis (1885-1959), William A. Dillon (1877-1966) m. Albert von Tilzer (1878-1956)

My Mammy (1920) w. Sam M. Lewis (1885-1959), Joe Young (1889-1939) m. Walter Donaldson (1893-1947) (M) Sinbad (F) The Jazz Singer, Rose of Washington Square, The Jolson Story, Jolson Sings Again

My Man (1921) w. English: Channing Pollock (1880-1946) w. French: Albert Willemetz (1887-1964), Jacques Charles (1882-1971) m. Maurice Yvain (1891-1965). Theme song of Fanny Brice. (M) Ziegfeld Follies of 1921 (F) My Man, The Great Ziegfeld, Rose of Washington Square, Funny Girl, Lady Sings the Blues

My Melancholy Baby (1912) w. George A. Norton (1880-1923) m. Ernie Burnett (1884-1959). Theme song of Tommy Lyman. (F) Birth of the Blues, Both Ends of the Candle

My Mother's Rosary (1915) w. Sam M. Lewis (1885-1959) m. George W. Meyer (1884-1959)

My Object All Sublime (1885) From the operetta, "The Mikado." w. W.S. Gilbert (1836-1911) m. Arthur Sullivan (1842-1900)

My Old Kentucky Home (1853) w.m. Stephen Foster (1826-1864). (F) Swanee River, I Dream Of Jeannie

My Pony Boy (1908/09) w. Bobby Heath (1889/90-1952) m. Charles O'Donnell. (M) Miss Innocence

My Sweetheart's the Man in the Moon (1892) w.m. James Thornton (1861-1938)

My Wife Won't Let Me (Waiting at the Church) (1906) w. Fred W. Leigh (? -1924 P) m. Henry E. Pether (? -1932 P). (F) Birth of the Blues

My Wild Irish Rose (1899) w.m. Chauncey Olcott (1858-1932). (F) My Wild Irish Rose

National Emblem March (When/and the monkey wrapped his tail around the flagpole) (1906) m. E.E. Bagley (1857-1922). Performed at circuses.

Neapolitan Love Song (1915) w. Henry Blossom (1866-1919) m. Victor Herbert (1859-1924). (M) The Princess Pat (F) The Great Victor Herbert

Nearer, My God, to Thee (1859) w. Sarah F. Adams (1805-1834) m. Lowell Mason (1792-1872)

Nelly Bly (1849) w.m. Stephen Foster (1826-1864)

Nelly Was a Lady (1849) w.m. Stephen Foster (1826-1864)

New World Symphony (1894) m. Antonin Dvorák (1841-1904) (Op. 95)

New York Hippodrome March (1915) m. John Philip Sousa (1854-1932)

Night on Bald Mountain (1886/88/ published after Mussorgsky's death) Symphonic poem. m. Modeste Mussorgsky (1839-1881). (F) Fantasia

Ninety-Nine Bottles of Beer on the Wall Traditional

Nobody Knows the Trouble I've Seen (1867) Traditional Black American. *Henry (aka Harry) Thacker (H.T.) Burleigh (1866/86-1949) did arrangements of many traditional spirituals and popularized them in the early decades of the 1900's. The arrangement of this song done by H.T. Burleigh is in the Public Domain.*

Nocturne Op. 9, No. 2 (1832?) m. Fréderic Chopin (1810-1849)

Now I Lay Me Down to Sleep (1894) From the opera, "Hansel and Gretel." w. Adelheid Wette (1858-1916) m. Engelbert Humperdinck (1854-1921). Also known as "Evening Prayer."

Now the Day is Over (1869) w. Rev. Sabine Baring-Gould (1834-1924) m. J. (Joseph) Barnby (1838-1896)

Nozze di Figaro, Le (1786) Opera. w. Lorenzo Da Ponte (1749-1838) m. W.A. Mozart (1756-1791). Very popular overture.

Nutcracker Suite, The (1892) From the ballet, "The Nutcracker." m. Peter I. Tchaikovsky (1840-1893). Contains many popular Christmas melodies. (F) Fantasia

O (Ach) Du Lieber Augustin (Polly [Molly] Put the Kettle On) (Did You Ever See a Lassie?) (m. 1788/89? w. 1800?)

O Come All Ye Faithful (Adeste Fideles) (1700's) Traditional Christmas carol. w. Latin: John Francis Wade (1710/11-1786) w. English: Frederick Oakeley (1802-1880) m. John Francis Wade (1710/11-1786)

O Come, O Come, Emmanuel Traditional Christmas carol. w. Latin: Anonymous w. English: Rev. John Mason Neale (1818-1866) m. Anonymous. *There are many different English translations of this song written at different times. If you are using an English translation, make sure it is in the Public Domain. The John Mason Neale translation, which is one of the best known, is Public Domain.*

O God, Our Help in Ages Past (1719/37/38) w. Isaac Watts (1674-1748) m. William Croft (1678-1727)

O Holy Night (Cantique de Noël) (1847/58) Traditional Christmas carol. w. French: Placide Cappeau (1808-1877) w. English: John Sullivan Dwight (1813/18-1893) m. Adolphe-Charles Adam (1803-1856)

O Little Town of Bethlehem (1868) Traditional Christmas carol. w. Phillips Brooks (1835-1893) m. L. H. Redner (1831-1908)

'O Sole Mio (1899) w. G. Capurro (1859-1920 S) m. E. di Capua (1864-1917 S). *The songs, "There's No Tomorrow," by Hoffman, Corday, and Carr, and "It's Now or Never" by Aaron Schroeder and Wally Gold, are both based on this song. "There's No Tomorrow" and "It's Now or Never" are* **not** *Public Domain. Note: The Italian performing rights society (SIAE) has informed us of a current lawsuit involving Emmanuele (Alfredo) Mazzucchi (1879-1972 S) regarding ownership of this song. This could affect the song's status outside the U.S. It will remain PD in the United States.*

O Tännenbaum, O Tännenbaum Traditional German Christmas carol. *This song is known in English as "O Christmas Tree," and there seem to be many English translations, written at different times. If you are using an English translation, make sure it is in the Public Domain. You can check with BZ/Rights Stuff about this.*

Oceana Roll, The (1911) w. Roger Lewis (1885-1948 A) m. Lucien Denni (1886/87-1947). (F) Mildred Pierce

Ode to Joy (1826) From Symphony No. 9. w. Friedrich Schiller (1759-1805) m. Ludwig van Beethoven (1770-1827). Famous last movement, for vocal soloists, chorus and orchestra (Op. 125). (F) Help!, A Clockwork Orange

Oh! By Jingo, Oh! By Gee, You're the Only Girl for Me (1919) w. Lew Brown (1893-1958) m. Albert von Tilzer (1878-1956). (M) Linger Longer Letty, (F) Incendiary Blonde, Skirts Ahoy

Oh! Dear, What Can the Matter Be? (1700's) Traditional English

Oh Dem Golden Slippers (Golden Slippers) (1879) w.m. James A. Bland (1854-1911). (F) Tulsa Kid

Oh, Didn't It Rain (1919) Traditional Black American. *Henry (aka Harry) Thacker (H.T.) Burleigh (1866/86-1949) did arrangements of many traditional spirituals and popularized them in the early decades of the 1900's. The arrangement of this song by H.T. Burleigh is in the Public Domain. There is a 1923 song with this same title credited to Eddie Leonard. The Eddie Leonard song is **not** in the Public Domain.*

Oh! How I Hate to Get Up in the Morning (1918) w.m. Irving Berlin (1888-1989). World War I song. (M) Yip! Yip! Yaphank, This Is the Army (F) Alexander's Ragtime Band, This Is the Army

Oh! How She Could Yacki, Hacki, Wicki, Wacki, Woo (1916) w. Charles McCarron (1891-1919 A), Stanley Murphy (1875-1919 A) m. Albert von Tilzer (1878-1956)

Oh Johnny, Oh Johnny, Oh (1917) w. Ed Rose (1875-1935) m. Abe Olman (1888-1984). (M) Follow Me

Oh, My Darling Clementine (Clementine) (1884/85) Traditional American. *The 1960 Woody Harris adaptation of this song is **not** Public Domain.*

Oh Promise Me (1889/90) w. Clement Scott (1841-1904) m. Reginald De Koven (1859-1920). (M) Robin Hood

Oh! Susanna (1848) w.m. Stephen Foster (1826-1864). (F) Swanee River, Colorado, Overland Telegraph, I Dream Of Jeannie

Oh! What a Pal Was Mary (1919) w. Bert Kalmar (1884-1947), Edgar Leslie (1885-1976) m. Pete Wendling (1888-1974 A), arrangement by Fred E. Ahlert (1892-1953 A). *The 1919 arrangement by Fred E. Ahlert is in the Public Domain in the United States.*

Oh Where, Oh Where Has My Little Dog Gone (1864) Traditional, originally German. w. English: Septimus Winner (1827-1902) m. Traditional

Oh, You Beautiful Doll (1911) w. A. Seymour Brown (1885-1947 A) m. Nat D. Ayer (1887-1952). (F) Wharf Angel, The Story of Vernon and Irene Castle, For Me and My Gal, Oh You Beautiful Doll

Old Black Joe (1860) w.m. Stephen Foster (1826-1864). (F) Swanee River

Old Dan Tucker (1843) w.m. Daniel Decatur Emmett (1815-1904)

Old Dog Tray (1852/53) w.m. Stephen Foster (1826-1864). (F) I Dream of Jeannie

Old-Fashioned Garden (1919) w.m. Cole Porter (1891/92-1964). (M) Hitchy-Koo of 1919 (F) Night and Day

Old Fashioned Wife, An (1917) w. P.G. Wodehouse (1881-1975) m. Jerome Kern (1885-1945). (M) Oh, Boy!

Old Folks at Home (Way Down Upon the Swanee River) (1851) w.m. Stephen Foster (1826-1864). (F) I Dream Of Jeannie.

Old Grey Mare (1858/1917) Traditional American

Old Hundred(th) Doxology (Praise God From Whom All Blessings Flow) (1500's) w. Psalm 134 of the Genevan Psalter. m. Louis Bourgeois (1510?-15??)

Old King Cole Traditional Mother Goose children's song

Old MacDonald Had a Farm Traditional children's song

Old Oaken Bucket, The (1800's) w. Samuel Woodworth (1784/85-1842) m. George Kiallmark

Old Rugged Cross, The (1913) w.m. Reverend George Bennard (1873-1958)

On a Sunday Afternoon (1902) w. Andrew B. Sterling (1874-1955) m. Harry von Tilzer (1872-1946). (F) Atlantic City, The Naughty Nineties

On the Banks of the Wabash Far Away (1899) w.m. Paul Dresser (1857-1906). (F) My Gal Sal, The Jolson Story, Wait Till the Sun Shines Nellie

On the Beach at Waikiki (1915) w. G.H. Stover m. Henry Kailimai. (M) The Bird of Paradise

On the 5:15 (1914) w. Stanley Murphy (1875-1919 A) m. Henry I. Marshall (1883-1958). (M) 5064 Gerard

On the Road to Mandalay (1907) w. Rudyard Kipling (1865-1936) m. Oley Speaks (1874-1948)

On Top of Old Smokey Traditional American. (F) Valley Of Fire. *New words were written for this song, and it was renamed, "On Top of Spaghetti." The words to "On Top of Spaghetti" are* **not** *Public Domain.*

On Wisconsin (1909) School Song of the University of Wisconsin. w. Carl Beck (1886-1965) m. W.T. Purdy (1882-1918/19)

Onward, Christian Soldiers (1864/71) w. Rev. Sabine Baring-Gould (1834-1924) m. Arthur Sullivan (1842-1900)

Otchi Tchorniya (Translated as Dark Eyes) (1884) Traditional Russian. *There is another song entitled "Dark Eyes" or "Black Eyes" written in 1926 by Harry Horlick and Gregory Stone. The Horlick/Stone song is* **not** *in the Public Domain.*

Otello (1887) Opera. w. A. Boito (1842-1918) m. Giuseppe Verdi (1813-1901)

Out Where the West Begins (1917) w. Arthur Chapman m. Estelle Philleo

Over There (1917) w.m. George M. Cohan (1878-1942). World War I song. (M) Zig-Zag, George M! (F) The Cockeyed World, Yankee Doodle Dandy

Pachelbel's Canon (1600's) m. Johann Pachelbel (1653-1706).
(F) Ordinary People

Pack Up Your Troubles in Your Old Kit-Bag (1915) w. George Asaf (1880-1951) m. Felix Powell (1878-1942). World War I song. (M) Her Soldier Boy, Dancin' (F) It's a Great Life. Wait Till the Sun Shines Nellie, On Moonlight Bay

Palm Leaf Rag (1903) m. Scott Joplin (1868-1919)

Paloma, La (The Dove) (1859) w.m. Sebastian Yradier (1809-1865)

Parade of the Wooden Soldiers (m. 1905/11? w. English 1922) m. Léon Jessel (1871-1942) w. English: Ballard MacDonald (1882-1935 A)

Patapan Traditional Christmas carol

Pease Porridge Hot Traditional Mother Goose children's song

Peer Gynt (1874/75) Orchestral suite. m. Edvard Grieg (1843-1907) (Op. 23)

Peg o' My Heart (1913) w. Alfred Bryan (1871-1958 A) m. Fred Fisher (1875-1942). (M) The Ziegfeld Follies of 1913 (F) Oh You Beautiful Doll

Perfect Day, A (1910) w.m. Carrie Jacobs-Bond (1862-1946)

Peter Peter Pumpkin Eater Traditonal Mother Goose children's song

Piano Concerto No. 1 (1875/80) m. Peter I. Tchaikovsky (1840-1893). Famous opening theme.

Please Go 'Way and Let Me Sleep (1902) w.m. J. Tim Bryman (1879-1946 A). Used in the silent movie era for scenes where someone desperately needs help and frantically tries to wake someone.

Poet and Peasant Overture (1854) m. Franz von Suppé (1819-1895)

Polly (Molly) Put the Kettle On (O [Ach] Du Lieber Augustin) (Did You Ever See a Lassie?) (m. 1788/89? w. 1809/10)

Polly-Wolly-Doodle Traditional Black American. (F) Tangier

Polonaise in A-flat (1843) m. Fréderic Chopin (1810-1849) (Op. 53)

Polonaise Militaire (1840) m. Fréderic Chopin (1810-1849) (Op. 40)

Polovetsian Dances (1888/ "Prince Igor" was completed after Borodin's death) From the opera, "Prince Igor." m. Alexander Borodin (1833-1887). *The musical, "Kismet" used melodies from the "Polovetsian Dances." The music from "Kismet" is* **not** *Public Domain.*

Pomp and Circumstance (1901/02) From "Military Marches for Full Orchestra." m. Edward Elgar (1857-1934) (Op. 39, No. 1). Often played at graduations.

Poor Butterfly (1916) w. John L. Golden (1874-1955) m. Raymond Hubbell (1879-1954). (M) The Big Show

Pop Goes the Weasel Children's song. w. Traditional American m. Traditional English

Praise God From Whom All Blessings Flow (Old Hundred[th] Doxology) (1500's) w. Psalm 134 of the Genevan Psalter m. Louis Bourgeois (1510?-15??)

Prayer of Thanksgiving (We Gather Together) Traditional Dutch hymn. English translation by Theodore Baker (185?-1934).

Prelude (1839) m. Fréderic Chopin (1810-1849) (Op. 28, No. 7)

Pretty Baby (1916) w. Gus Kahn (1886-1941) m. Tony Jackson (1876-1921), Egbert van Alstyne (1882-1951). (M) The Passing Show of 1916, Houp-La (F) Rose of Washington Square, I'll See You In My Dreams, The Eddie Cantor Story

Pretty Girl is Like a Melody, A (1919) w.m. Irving Berlin (1888-1989). (M) Ziegfeld Follies of 1919 (F) The Great Ziegfeld, Alexander's Ragtime Band, Blue Skies, There's No Business Like Show Business

Prince of Denmark's March (1702) Celebrated trumpet piece. m. Jeremiah Clarke (1674-1707). *This work has long been thought to be by Henry Purcell and was simply called "Trumpet Voluntary," but it is actually by Jeremiah Clarke and bears the title, "Prince of Denmark's March."*

Put On Your Old Grey Bonnet (1909) w. Stanley Murphy (1875-1919 A) m. Percy Wenrich (1880/87-1952)

Put Your Arms Around Me, Honey (Hold me tight) (1910) w. Junie McCree (1865-1918) m. Albert von Tilzer (1878-1956). (F) Coney Island, Louisiana Hayride, In the Good Old Summertime

Ragging the Scale (1915) m. Edward B. Claypoole (1883-1952 A)

Ragtime Cowboy Joe (1912) w.m. Lewis F. Muir (1884-1950), Grant Clarke (1891-1931), Maurice Abrahams (1883-1931 A). (F) Hello Frisco Hello, Incendiary Blonde

Red River Valley, The (1896) w.m. Anonymous. Song refers to the Red River in Manitoba, Canada. (F) The Grapes of Wrath, King of the Cowboys

Reflection Rag (1917/18) m. Scott Joplin (1868-1919)

Reveille (1836) Traditional French-American bugle call

Reverie (1890/91) m. Claude Debussy (1862-1918)

Rheingold, Das (1853/54) Opera. w.m. Richard Wagner (1813-1883). One of four operas that comprise Der Ring des Nibelungen.

Ride of the Valkyries (1863/65) From the opera, "Die Walküre." m. Richard Wagner (1813-1883)

Rigoletto (1852) Opera. w. F.M. Piave (1810-1876) m. Giuseppe Verdi (1813-1901)

Ring Around the (a) Rosie Traditional children's song

Ring des Nibelungen, Der Opera tetralogy. w.m. Richard Wagner (1813-1883). Consists of four operas: Das Rheingold (1853/54); Die Walküre (1854/56); Siegfried (1856/71); Götterdämmerung (1873/74)

Roamin' in the Gloamin' (1911) w.m. Harry Lauder (1870-1950)

Rock of Ages (1832) w. Augustus Montague Toplady (1740-1778) m. Thomas Hastings (1784-1872)

Rock-a-Bye Baby (1765? words/ 1862 music) w. Traditional Mother Goose. m. Effie I. Crockett

Rock-a-Bye Your Baby with a Dixie Melody (1918) w. Sam M. Lewis (1885-1959), Joe Young (1889-1939) m. Jean Schwartz (1878-1956). (M) Sinbad (F) Show of Shows, Rose of Washington Square, The Jolson Story, Jolson Sings Again, The Merry Monahans

Rocked in the Cradle of the Deep (1840) w. Mrs. Willard m. Joseph P. Knight (1812-1887)

Romance (1859) m. Anton Rubinstein (1829/30-1894). *There are many songs titled "Romance." Only the Rubinstein version is Public Domain.*

Rosary, The (1898) w. Robert Cameron Rogers (1862-1912) m. Ethelbert Nevin (1862-1901)

Rose of Sharon, The (1884) w.m. Alexander Campbell Mackenzie (1847-1935)

Rose of the Rio Grande (1922) w. Edgar Leslie (1885-1976) m. Harry Warren (1893-1981), Ross Gorman. (M) The 1940's Radio Hour

Rose of Washington Square (1919) w. Ballard MacDonald (1882-1935 A) m. James F. Hanley (1892-1942 A). Theme song of Fanny Brice. (M) Ziegfeld Midnight Frolic (F) Rose of Washington Square.

Roses of Picardy (1916) w. Frederick E. Weatherly (1848-1929) m. Haydn Wood (?-1959 P). American song popular during World War I; Picardy is a region in France.

'Round Her Neck She Wears (Wore) a Yellow (Yeller) Ribbon (She Wore a Yellow Ribbon) (1917) w.m. George A. Norton (1880-1923) *It is probable this was an early American folk song. A well-known version, credited to George A. Norton, was registered at the U.S. Copyright Office in 1917. There are updated and arranged versions of this song, so be extremely careful to use the Norton version, or an even earlier one.* (F) She Wore a Yellow Ribbon

Row, Row, Row (And then he'd) (1912) w. William Jerome (1865-1932 A) m. James V. Monaco (1885-1945). (M) Ziegfeld Follies of 1912 (F) Incendiary Blonde, The Eddie Cantor Story, The Seven Little Foys

Row, Row, Row Your Boat Traditional. Children's song/round

Royal Fireworks Music (1749) m. George Frederick Handel (1685-1759)

Rule Britannia (1740/41) w. David Mallet (1705?-1765) or James Thomson (1700-1748) m. Thomas Augustine Arne (1710-1778) .

Runnin' Wild (1922) w. Joe Grey (1879/80-1956), Leo Wood (1882-1929) m. A. Harrington Gibbs (1896-1956), arrangement by Joe Grey (1879/80-1956). (F) Running Wild, Some Like It Hot, The Five Pennies. *The 1922 arrangement by Joe Grey is in the Public Domain in the United States.*

Sailing (Sailing, sailing over the bounding main) (1880) w.m. Godfrey Marks

Sailor's Hornpipe (1775?) Traditional English

Sally (1921) w. Clifford Grey (1887-1941) m. Jerome Kern (1885-1945). (M) Sally (F) Sally

Santa Lucia (1849/50) Popular Neopolitan song. w.m. T. Cottrau (1827-1879). (F) A Night at the Opera

Say It with Music (1921) w.m. Irving Berlin (1888-1989). Theme song of Jack Payne. (M) Music Box Revue, Mayfair and Montmartre (F) Alexander's Ragtime Band

Scarborough Fair (1800's) Anonymous British. *The Simon & Garfunkel version of this song is **not** Public Domain.*

Scheherazade (1890) Symphonic suite. m. Nikolai Rimsky-Korsakov (1844-1908)

School Days (1906/07) w.m. Will D. Cobb (1876-1930), Gus Edwards (1879-1945)

Searchlight Rag (1907) m. Scott Joplin (1868-1919)

Seasons, The (1798/1801) w.m. Franz Joseph Haydn (1732-1809)

Second Hand Rose (1921) w. Grant Clarke (1891-1931) m. James F. Hanley (1892-1942 A). (M) Ziegfeld Follies of 1921 (F) My Man

See Saw, Margery Daw Traditional Mother Goose children's song

Semper Fidelis (1888) March. m. John Philip Sousa (1854-1932). (F) The Cockeyed World

She is More to Be Pitied Than Censured (1884) w.m. William B. Gray (?-1932)

Sheik of Araby, The (1921) w. Harry B. Smith (1860-1936), Francis Wheeler m. Ted Snyder (1881-1965). (M) Make It Snappy (F) Tin Pan Alley

Shenandoah (Across the Wide Missouri) (1800's) Traditional American

Shine On, Harvest Moon (1908) w. Jack Norworth (1879-1959) m. Nora Bayes-Norworth (1880-1928). (M) Ziegfeld Follies, Miss Innocence (F) Ever Since Eve, Nancy Goes to Rio, Shine On Harvest Moon, The Eddy Duchin Story

Shoo Fly, Don't Bother Me (1869?) Traditional American. w. Billy Reeves (1943-) m. Frank Campbell

Shuffle Along (1921) w.m. Noble Sissle (1889-1975 A), Eubie Blake (1883-1983 A). (M) Shuffle Along, Eubie!

Sidewalks of New York, The (East Side, West Side) (1894) w.m. Charles B. Lawlor (1852-1925), James W. Blake (1862-1935). (F) Beau James

Siegfried (1856/71) Opera. w.m. Richard Wagner (1813-1883). One of four operas that comprise Der Ring des Nibelungen.

Silent Night (1818) Traditional Christmas carol. w. German: Joseph Mohr (1792-1848) w. English: John Freeman Young (1820-1885), m. Franz Gruber (1787-1863)

Silver Sails (1914) w. Edward Chevalier (1886-1968) m. Geoffrey Smitham (1888-1952)

Silver Threads Among the Gold (1873) w. Eben E. Rexford (184?-1916) m. H.P. Danks (1834-1903)

Simple Melody (1914) w.m. Irving Berlin (1888-1989). (M) Watch Your Step (F) There's No Business Like Show Business. *The Public Domain version of this song is the song as it was used in the stage musical comedy, "Watch Your Step." Berlin copyrighted a new piano arrangement of this song in 1950. The 1950 piano arrangement, which he called "Play A Simple Melody," is* **not** *Public Domain.*

Sing a Song of Sixpence Traditional Mother Goose children's song

Sipping Cider Thru' a Straw (1919) w.m. Lee David (1891-1978 A), Carey
 Morgan (1885-1960 A)

Skaters' Waltz (1882) m. Emile Waldteufel (1837-1915)

Skip to My Lou Traditional American. (F) Meet Me in St. Louis, The Searchers

Slavonic Dances (1878) m. Antonin Dvořák (1841-1904) (Op. 46)

Sleeping Beauty (1889/90) Ballet. m. Peter I. Tchaikovsky (1840-1893) (Op. 66).
 (F) The Gold Rush

Smile the While You Kiss Me Sad Adieu (Till We Meet Again) (1918)
 w. Raymond B. Egan (1890-1952) m. Richard A. Whiting (1891-1938). (F) On
 Moonlight Bay, The Eddy Duchin Story

Smiles (There are smiles that make us happy) (1917) w. J. Will Callahan
 (1874-1946) m. Lee S. Roberts (1884-1949). (M) The Passing Show of 1918 (F) The
 Dolly Sisters, Somebody Loves Me, Wait Till the Sun Shines Nellie, The Eddy
 Duchin Story

Smilin' Through (1918/19) w.m. Arthur A. Penn (1875/76-1941). (F) Smilin' Through

Snookey Ookums (1913) w.m. Irving Berlin (1888-1989). (M) Hullo Ragtime
 (F) Easter Parade

Solace (1909) m. Scott Joplin (1868-1919)

So Long Oo-Long, How Long You Gonna Be Gone? (1920) w.m. Bert
 Kalmar (1884-1947), Harry Ruby (1895-1974). (F) Three Little Words

Some of These Days (1910) w.m. Shelton Brooks (1886-1975 A), based on Frank Williams' "Some o' Dese Days." Theme song of Sophie Tucker.
(F) Animal Crackers, Broadway, Follow the Boys

Some Sunday Morning (1917) w. Gus Kahn (1886-1941), Raymond B. Egan (1890-1952) m. Richard A. Whiting (1891-1938). *There is a song written in 1945 by Koehler, Jerome, and Heindorf, that has the same title. The 1945 song is **not** Public Domain.*

Somebody Stole My Gal (1918) w.m. Leo Wood (1882-1929). Theme song of Billy Cotton.

Sometime (1918) w. Rida Johnson Young (1869-1926) m. Rudolf Friml (1879-1972). (M) Sometime

Sometimes I Feel Like a Motherless Child Traditional Black American. *Henry (aka Harry) Thacker (H.T.) Burleigh (1866/86-1949) did arrangements of many traditional spirituals and popularized them in the early decades of the 1900's. The arrangement of this song done by H.T. Burleigh is in the Public Domain.*

Somewhere a Voice is Calling (1911) w. Eileen Newton m. Arthur F. Tate (? -1950 A & P)

Song of Love (1921) w. Dorothy Donnelly (1880-1928 A) m. Sigmund Romberg (1887-1951). (M) Blossom Time. *Based on the second theme of Schubert's "Unfinished Symphony" and on a melody by Heinrich Berté (1857/58-1924).*

Song of Songs, The (1914) w. French: Maurice Vaucaire (186?-1918) w. English: Clarence Lucas (1866-1947) m. Moya (?-1922) (Moya is a pseudonym of Harold Vicars)

Song of the Volga Boatmen (1800's) Traditional Russian

Songs My Mother Taught Me (1880) From "Gypsy Songs." w. Adolf Heyduk (1835-1923) m. Antonin Dvorák (1841-1904) (Op. 55)

Sorcerer's Apprentice, The (1897) Symphonic poem. m. Paul Dukas (1865-1935). (F) Fantasia

Souvenirs (1905) w. Judith Fontana (1871-1920) m. Charles Greene (1874-1937)

Spanish Moss (1903) w. Albert Owen (1876-1935) m. Gilbert Peele (1874-1942)

Spring is Everywhere (1917) w. Evelyn Cannon (1880-1949) m. Richard Starfield (1884-1957)

Spring Song (1844) From "Songs Without Words." m. Felix Mendelssohn (1809-1847) (Op. 62)

St. John Passion (1724) w.m. J.S. Bach (1685-1750)

St. Louis Blues (1914) w.m. W.C. Handy (1873-1958). (F) St. Louis Blues, Is Everybody Happy?, The Birth of the Blues

St. Matthew Passion (1727) w.m. J.S. Bach (1685-1750)

Star Spangled Banner, The (1780? music/1814 words) American National Anthem. w. Francis Scott Key (1779-1843) m. John Stafford Smith (1750-1836). Written during the bombardment of Ft. McHenry, 1814.

Stars and Stripes Forever (1897) March. m. John Philip Sousa (1854-1932). (M) Dancin'

Steal Away (1921) Traditional Black American. *Henry (aka Harry) Thacker (H.T.) Burleigh (1866/86-1949) did arrangements of many traditional spirituals and popularized them in the early decades of the 1900's. The arrangement of this song by H.T. Burleigh is in the Public Domain.*

Steamboat Bill (1910) w. Ren Shields (1868-1913) m. Bert Leighton (1877-1964 A), Frank Leighton. (F) Ridin' on a Rainbow

Streets of Cairo, The (Hootchy Kootchy Dance) (Oh they don't wear pants in the southern part of France) (1893/95) w.m. James Thornton (1861-1938)

Streets of Laredo (The Cowboy's Lament) (1800's) Traditional American. (F) Streets of Laredo, Utah Wagon Train. *There is a 1948 version of this song, by Ray Evan and Jay Livingston, that is **not** Public Domain.*

Streets of New York, The (In Old New York) (1906) w. Henry Blossom (1866-1919) m. Victor Herbert (1859-1924). (M) The Red Mill

Stumbling (1922) w.m. Edward E. (Zez) Confrey (1895-1971)

Sugar Blues (1919) w. Lucy Fletcher m. Clarence Williams (1893/98-1965)

Sunbonnet Sue (1906/08) w. Will D. Cobb (1876-1930) m. Gus Edwards (1879-1945). (F) The Star Maker, Sunbonnet Sue

Sunshine of Your Smile, The (1915) w. Leonard Cooke (? -1919 P) m. Lillian Ray (? -1949 A & P) (Lillian Ray is a pseudonym of John Neat)

Sur le Pont d'Avignon (1846) Traditional French children's song

Swan Lake (1875/76/77) Ballet. m. Peter I. Tchaikovsky (1840-1893)

Swanee (1919) w. Irving Caesar (1895-   ) m. George Gershwin (1898-1937). (M) Sinbad, The Glorious Days. (F) Rhapsody in Blue, The Jolson Story, Jolson Sings Again, A Star Is Born

Sweet Adeline (1903) w. Richard H. Gerard (1876-1948) m. Henry W. Armstrong (1879-1951). Popular barbershop-quartet song.

Sweet and Low (1863) w. Alfred Tennyson (1809-1892) m. J. (Joseph) Barnby (1838-1896)

Sweet Betsy from Pike (1800's) Traditional British/American

Sweet Little Buttercup (1917) w. Alfred Bryan (1871-1958 A) m. Herman Paley (1879-1955)

Sweet Molly Malone (Cockles and Mussels) Traditional Irish

Sweet Rosie O'Grady (1896) w.m. Maude Nugent (187?-1958)

Sweetheart of Sigma Chi, The (1912) Fraternity song. w. Byron D. Stokes (1886-1974 A) m. F. Dudleigh Vernor (1892-1974 A). (F) The Sweetheart of Sigma Chi

Sweethearts (1913) w. Robert B. Smith (1875-1951) m. Victor Herbert (1859-1924). (M) Sweethearts (F) Sweethearts

Swing Low, Sweet Chariot Traditional Black American. *Henry (aka Harry) Thacker (H.T.) Burleigh (1866/86-1949) did arrangements of many traditional spirituals and popularized them in the early decades of the 1900's. The arrangement of this song done by H.T. Burleigh is in the Public Domain.* (M) Bubbling Brown Sugar

Sycamore, The (1904) m. Scott Joplin (1868-1919)

Sylvia (1914) w. Clinton Scollard (1860-1932) m. Oley Speaks (1874-1948)

Sympathy (1912) w. Otto Harbach (1873-1963) m. Rudolf Friml (1879-1972). (M) The Firefly (F) The Firefly

Symphony No. 1 (1877) m. Johannes Brahms (1833-1897). Well-known main theme from last movement (Op. 68).

Symphony No. 3 ("Eroica") (1806/09) m. Ludwig van Beethoven (1770-1827) (Op. 55)

Symphony No. 5 (1809) m. Ludwig van Beethoven (1770-1827). "Fate knocking at the door" (first movement main theme) (Op. 67)

Symphony No. 6 ("Pastorale") (1809) m. Ludwig van Beethoven (1770-1827) (Op. 68)

Symphony No. 9 ("Choral") (1826) m. Ludwig van Beethoven (1770-1827). "Ode to Joy" (last movement) (Op. 125)

Ta-Ra-Ra Boom-De-Ay (1891) w.m. Henry J. Sayers (1855-1932)

Take Me Out to the Ball Game (1908) w. Jack Norworth (1879-1959) m. Albert von Tilzer (1878-1956). (F) Everybody's Cheering

Tales from the Vienna Woods (1868) Waltz. m. Johann Strauss, Jr. (1825-1899) (Op. 325). (F) The Great Waltz

Taps (1862) Bugle call. m. Gen. Daniel O. Butterfield (1831-1901). Sounded in the Army at the end of each day, as the flag is lowered.

Teddy Bears' Picnic, The (1907) m. John W. Bratton (1867-1947 A) *Only the music of this song is in Public Domain.* The words, written in 1948 by Jimmy M. Kennedy (1902-1984), are still under copyright.

Ten Little Indians (Injuns) (1868) w.m. Septimus Winner (1827-1902)

Tenting on the Old Camp Ground (Tenting tonight) (1864) w.m. Walter Kittredge (1834-1905)

That Old Irish Mother of Mine (1920) w. William Jerome (1865-1932) m. Harry von Tilzer (1872-1946)

That Tumble-Down Shack in Athlone (1918) w. Richard W. Pascoe (1888-1968 A) m. Monte Carlo (1883-1967 A), Alma M. Sanders (1882-1956 A)

That Wonderful Mother of Mine (1918) w. Clyde Hager (1886-1944 A) m. Walter Goodwin (1889-1966 A)

That's an Irish Lullaby (Too-Ra-Loo-Ra-Loo-Ral, That's an Irish Lullaby)
(1914) w.m. James Royce Shannon (1881-1946 A). (M) Shameen Dhu (F) Going My
Way

There is a Tavern in the Town (1883) Traditional American

There'll Be a Hot Time in the Old Town Tonight (1896) w. Joseph Hayden (? -1937)
m. Theodore A. Metz (1848-1936). (M) Me and Bessie

There'll Be Some Changes Made (1921) w. William (Billy) Higgins m. W. Benton
Overstreet. Arrangement by Fletcher Hamilton Henderson, Jr. *The arrangement of
this song by Fletcher Hamilton Henderson, Jr. is in the Public Domain.* (M) Bubbling
Brown Sugar (F) Designing Woman

There's a Broken Heart For Every Light on Broadway (1915)
w. Howard Johnson (1887-1941 A) m. Fred Fisher (1875-1942). (F) Oh You
Beautiful Doll

There's a Long, Long Trail (1913/14) Popular British song during World War I.
w. Stoddard King (1889-1933 A) m. Zo Elliott (1891-1964)

There's a Quaker Down in Quaker Town (1916) w. David Berg (1892-1944 A)
m. Alfred Solman (1868-1937)

They Didn't Believe Me (1914) w. Herbert Reynolds (1867-1933)
m. Jerome Kern (1885-1945). (M) The Girl From Utah (F) Tonight's the Night, Till the
Clouds Roll By, That Midnight Kiss

They Go Wild Simply Wild Over Me (1917) w. Joseph McCarthy (1885-1943)
m. Fred Fisher (1875-1942)

Thine Alone (1917) w. Henry Blossom (1866-1919) m. Victor Herbert (1859-1924). (M)
Eileen (F) The Great Victor Herbert

This Old Man Traditional English children's song. *This song was adapted by Malcolm Arnold for use in the film, "The Inn of the Sixth Happiness." Arnold's adaptation is* **not** *Public Domain.*

Three Blind Mice (1609) Traditional children's song

Three Little Kittens Traditional Mother Goose children's song

Three Little Maids from School (1885) From the operetta, "The Mikado."
w. W.S. Gilbert (1836-1911) m. Arthur Sullivan (1842-1900)

Three O'Clock in the Morning (1921) w. Dorothy Terriss (1890-1953) (Dorothy Terriss is one of the pseudonyms for Theodora Morse) m. Julian Robledo (1887-1940). (F) Margie, Belles on Their Toes, The Eddy Duchin Story

Throw Me a Rose (1915/16) w. P.G. Wodehouse (1881-1975), Herbert Reynolds (1867-1933) m. Emmerich Kalman (1882-1953 A). (M) Little Miss Springtime

Thunderer, The (1889) March. m. John Philip Sousa (1854-1932)

Tiger Rag (Hold That Tiger!) (1917) m. The Original Dixieland Jazz Band.
(F) Is Everybody Happy, The Big Broadcast, Birth of the Blues, Has Anybody Seen My Gal, Night Club Girl. *Only the instrumental version of this selection is in the Public Domain.*

There are words to "Tiger Rag" by Harry DeCosta. The DeCosta words are **not** *Public Domain. The version that is in the Public Domain is the one by The Original Dixieland Jazz Band.*

Till the Clouds Roll By (1917) w. P.G. Wodehouse (1881-1975) m. Jerome Kern (1885-1945). (M) Oh Boy!, Oh Joy (F) Till the Clouds Roll By

Till We Meet Again (Smile the While You Kiss Me Sad Adieu) (1918)
w. Raymond B. Egan (1890-1952) m. Richard A. Whiting (1891-1938).
(F) On Moonlight Bay, The Eddy Duchin Story

'Tis Me Oh Lord, Standin' in de Need of Pray'r Traditional Black American. *Henry (aka Harry) Thacker (H.T.) Burleigh (1866/86-1949) did arrangements of many traditional spirituals and popularized them in the early decades of the 1900's. The arrangement of this song done by H.T. Burleigh is in the Public Domain.*

'Tis the Last Rose of Summer (1813) w. Thomas Moore (1779-1852) m. Based on "The Groves of Blarney," a traditional Irish song.

To a Wild Rose (1896) From "Woodland Sketches" for piano. m. Edward A. MacDowell (1861-1908) (Op. 51)

Too-Ra-Loo-Ra-Loo-Ral, That's an Irish Lullaby (That's an Irish Lullaby) (1914) w.m. James Royce Shannon (1881-1946 A). (M) Shameen Dhu (F) Going My Way

Toot, Toot, Tootsie! (Goo' Bye) (1922) w.m. Ernie Erdman (1879-1946), Ted Fiorito (1900-1971), Gilbert Keyes (1886-1941) (Gilbert Keyes is a pseudonym of Gus Kahn), Dan Russo (1925-1956 A). (M) Bombo (F) The Jazz Singer, Rose of Washington Square, The Jolson Story, Jolson Sings Again, I'll See You in My Dreams. *If you start researching this song, you will find that the names of the composers vary from reference book to reference book. The first registration for copyright for this song was made by Gilbert Keyes, Ernie Erdman, and Dan Russo. Renewal was done by the widow of Gus Kahn, the widow of Ernie Erdman, and Dan Russo himself. The renewal identifies Gilbert Keyes as a pseudonym of Gus Kahn. There is an assignment at the copyright office in which Ted Fiorito assigns certain rights in this song to Leo Feist (the music publisher).*

Toreador Song (1875) From the opera, "Carmen." w. H. Meilhac (1831-1897), L. Halévy (1834-1908) m. Georges Bizet (1838-1875)

Torna a Surriento! (1904) w. Giovanni Battista de Curtis (1860-1926 S) m. Ernesto de Curtis (1875-1937 S). (F) On the Sunny Side of the Street
If you are using an English translation of the words to this song, make sure the English translation is in the Public Domain.

Toyland (1903) w. Glen MacDonough (1870-1924 A) m. Victor Herbert. (1859-1924) (M) Babes In Toyland (F) Babes In Toyland

Trail of the Lonesome Pine, The (1913) w. Ballard MacDonald (1882-1935 A) m. Harry Carroll (1892-1962). (F) Way Out West

Tramp! Tramp! Tramp! (Along the highway) (1910) w. Rida Johnson Young (1869-1926) m. Victor Herbert (1859-1924). (M) Naughty Marietta (F) Naughty Marietta

Tramp, Tramp, Tramp (The boys are marching) (1864/65) w.m. George Frederick Root (1820-1895)

Traümerei (1839) From "Kinderscenen" ("Scenes from Childhood") for piano. m. Robert Schumann (1810-1856) (Op. 15, No.7)

Traviata, La (1853/54/55) Opera. w. F.M. Piave (1810-1876) m. Giuseppe Verdi (1813-1901)

Trees (1914/1922) w. Joyce Kilmer (1886-1918) m. Oscar (Otto) Rasbach (1889-1975). *"Trees" by Joyce Kilmer was first published as a poem in 1914, then set to music by Oscar Rasbach in 1922.*

Tristan und Isolde (1859/60) Opera. w.m. Richard Wagner (1813-1883)

Triumphal March (1871/72) From the opera, "Aida." m. Giuseppe Verdi (1813-1901)

Trout Quintet (1817/19) m. Franz Schubert (1797-1828)

Trumpet Voluntary (1702) Celebrated trumpet piece. m. Incorrectly attributed to Henry Purcell (1659-1695). *This work has long been thought to be by Henry Purcell and was simply called "Trumpet Voluntary," but it is actually by Jeremiah Clarke (1674-1707) and bears the title, "Prince of Denmark's March."*

Turkey in the Straw (1834) Traditional American folk melody, frequently played by country fiddlers.

Twelfth Street Rag (1914) m. Euday L. Bowman (1887-1949). *Only the music of this song is in the Public Domain.* However, several people have written lyrics for this song over the years, and *as not all of these lyrics are Public Domain*, they must be researched on a case-by-case basis.

Twelve Days of Christmas Traditional Christmas carol

Twinkle, Twinkle, Little Star Traditional children's song. w. Anonymous m. Same as "Alphabet Song," "Baa, Baa, Black Sheep."

Un Bel Di (1904) From the opera, "Madama Butterfly." w. Luigi Illica (1857-1919), Giuseppe Giacosa (1847-1906) m. Giacomo Puccini (1858-1924)

Under the Bamboo Tree (1902) w.m. Robert (Bob) Cole (1869-1911), J. Rosamond Johnson (1873-1954). (M) Sally in Our Alley (F) Meet Me in St. Louis

Unfinished Symphony (1866) m. Franz Schubert (1797-1828)

Up on the Housetop Traditional Christmas carol. w.m. Benjamin R. Hanby (1833-1867)

Valse Bleue (1900) Waltz. m. Alfred Margis (1874-1913)

Valse, La (1920) m. Maurice Ravel (1875-1937). Dance poem for orchestra. Often used for ballet performances.

Valse Tzigane (1904) m. F. D. Marchetti (? -1940 P). *In 1932, Dick Manning based his song "Fascination" on Marchetti's piece for café orchestra. Dick Manning's "Fascination" is* **not** *Public Domain.*

Vesti la Giubba (1892) From the opera, "I Pagliacci." w.m. Ruggiero Leoncavallo (1858-1919)

Vienna Life (Wiener Blut) (1873) Waltz. m. Johann Strauss, Jr. (1825-1899) (Op. 354)

Vissi d'Arte (1899) From the opera, "Tosca." w. V. Sardou (1831-1908), Luigi Illica (1857-1919), Giuseppe Giacosa (1847-1906), m. Giacomo Puccini (1858-1924)

Vive la Compagnie (1844) Traditional

Wabash Blues (1921) w. Dave Ringle (1895-1965) m. Fred Meinken (1883-1958). (F) Joan of the Ozarks

Wait for the Wagon (1851?) Traditional American

Wait Till the Cows Come Home (1917) w. Anne Caldwell (1867-1936) m. Ivan Caryll (1860/61-1921). (M) Jack O'Lantern

Wait Till the Sun Shines, Nellie (1905) w. Andrew B. Sterling (1874-1955) m. Harry von Tilzer (1872-1946). (F) Wait Till the Sun Shines Nellie, Birth of the Blues, In the Good Old Summertime

Waiting at the Church (My Wife Won't Let Me) (1906) w. Fred W. Leigh (? -1924 P) m. Henry E. Pether (? -1932 P). (F) Birth of the Blues

Waiting for the Robert E. Lee (1912) w. L. Wolfe Gilbert (1886-1970) m. Lewis F. Muir (1884-1950). (F) The Jolson Story, The Story of Vernon and Irene Castle

Walküre, Die (1854/56) Opera. w.m. Richard Wagner (1813-1883). One of four operas that comprise Der Ring des Nibelungen.

Waltz (1870) From the ballet, "Coppelia." m. Leo Delibes (1836-1891)

Waltz (1867) From the opera, "Romeo et Juliette." m. Charles Gounod (1818-1893)

Waltz Me Around Again Willie —'Round 'Round 'Round (1906) w. Will D. Cobb (1876-1930) m. Ren Shields (1868-1913). (M) His Honor the Mayor

Waltz of the Flowers (1892) From the ballet "The Nutcracker." m. Peter I. Tchaikovsky (1840-1893)

Wand'ring Minstrel, A (1885) From the operetta, "The Mikado." w. W.S. Gilbert (1836-1911) m. Arthur Sullivan (1842-1900)

Wang Wang Blues, The (1921) w. Leo Wood (1882-1929) m. Gus Mueller, Buster Johnson and Henry Busse (1894-1955). (F) Somebody Loves Me, The Rat Race

Washington Post March (1889/93) m. John Philip Sousa (1854-1932)

Wassail Song (Here We Go/Come A-Caroling/A-Wassailing) Traditional Christmas carol

Water Music (1733) Orchestral suite. m. George Frederick Handel (1685-1759)

Waves of the Danube (Danube Waves) (1880) Waltz. m. I. Ivanovici (1845-1902). *In 1947, Al Jolson and Saul Chaplin based their song "Anniversary Song," for the film, "The Jolson Story," on this music. "Anniversary Song" is* **not** *Public Domain.*

Way Down Upon the Swanee River (Old Folks at Home) (1851) w.m. Stephen Foster (1826-1864). (F) I Dream of Jeannie.

Way Down Yonder in New Orleans (1922) w.m. Henry Creamer (1879-1930), Turner Layton (1894-1978). (M) Spice of 1922 (F) Is Everybody Happy, Somebody Loves Me

We Gather Together (Prayer of Thanksgiving) Traditional Dutch hymn. English translation by Theodore Baker (185?-1934).

We Sail the Ocean Blue (1878) From the operetta, "H.M.S. Pinafore." w. W.S. Gilbert (1836-1911) m. Arthur Sullivan (1842-1900)

We Three Kings of Orient Are (1857/63) Traditional Christmas carol. w.m. John H. Hopkins (1820-1891)

We Wish You a Merry Christmas Traditional Christmas carol

Wearin' of the Green Traditional Irish

Wedding March (Here comes the bride) (1851/52) From the opera, "Lohengrin."
w.m. Richard Wagner (1813-1883)

Wedding March (Recessional) (1844) From the incidental music to "A Midsummer
Night's Dream." m. Felix Mendelssohn (1809-1847) (Op. 61)

Weeping Willow (1903) m. Scott Joplin (1868-1919)

Well-Tempered Clavier, The (1735/38/42) m. J. S. Bach (1685-1750).
Books I & II

We're Going Over (1917) w.m. Andrew B. Sterling (1874-1955), Bernie Grossman
(1885-1951 A), Arthur Lange (1889-1956 A). World War I song.

What a Friend We Have in Jesus (1876) Popular Protestant hymn. w. Horatius Bonar
(1808-1889) m. Charles Converse (1832-1918)

What Child is This? Traditional Christmas carol. w. William Chatterton Dix (1837-1898)
m. Same melody as "Greensleeves"

What Do You Want to Make Those Eyes at Me For (1916)
w.m. Joseph McCarthy (1885-1943), Howard Johnson (1887-1941 A),
James V. Monaco (1885-1945), **or** w. Joseph McCarthy (1885-1943),
Howard Johnson (1887-1941 A) m. James V. Monaco (1885-1945).
(M) The Better 'Ole (F) The Merry Monahans, Incendiary Blonde

When Hearts Are Young (1922) w. Cyrus Wood (1889-1942) m. Sigmund Romberg
(1887-1951), Alfred (Al) Goodman (1890-1972). (M) The Lady in Ermine

When I Leave the World Behind (1915) w.m. Irving Berlin (1888-1989)

When Irish Eyes Are Smiling (1912) w. Chauncey Olcott (1858-1932), George Graff, Jr. (1886-1973) m. Ernest R. Ball (1878-1927). (M) The Isle o' Dreams

When It's Apple Blossom Time in Normandy (1912) w.m. Harry Gifford (? -1960 P), Huntley Trevor (? -1943 P), Tom Mellor (? -1926 P). (F) Shine On Harvest Moon

When Johnny Comes Marching Home (1863) Famous Civil War song. w.m. Louis Lambert (1829-1892) (Louis Lambert is a pseudonym of Patrick Sarsfield Gilmore). (M) Dancin' (F) When Johnny Comes Marching Home. *There is an arrangement of this song by Buddy Kaye which was done in 1945. That arrangement is* **not** *Public Domain.*

When My Baby Smiles at Me (1920) w. Andrew B. Sterling (1874-1955), Ted Lewis (1891/92-1971) m. Bill Munro (1892-1969). (F) When My Baby Smiles at Me

When That Midnight Choo-Choo Leaves for Alabam' (1912) w.m. Irving Berlin (1888-1989). (F) Alexander's Ragtime Band, Easter Parade, There's No Business Like Show Business. *There is an arrangement of this song by Shipley Douglas entitled "When the Midnight Choo-Choo Leaves for Alabam" (with words and music by Irving Berlin) that is* **also** *in the Public Domain.*

When the Saints Go Marching In Traditional Black American. w. Katharine E. Purvis m. James M. Black

When You and I Were Young, Maggie (1866) w. George W. Johnson (1839-1917) m. James A. Butterfield (1837-1891). (F) Swing Time Johnny

When You Were Sweet Sixteen (1898) w.m. James Thornton (1861-1938). (F) A Man Called Sullivan, The Jolson Story

When You Wore a Tulip (And I wore a big red rose) (1914) w. Jack Mahoney (1882-1945) m. Percy Wenrich (1880/87-1952). (F) For Me and My Gal, Belles On Their Toes, The Merry Monahans

When You're a Long, Long Way from Home (1914) w. Sam M. Lewis (1885-1959) m. George W. Meyer (1884-1959)

When You're Away (Dear) (1914) w. Henry Blossom (1866-1919) m. Victor Herbert (1859-1924). (M) The Only Girl

When You're in Love with Someone Who is Not in Love with You (1915) w.m. Grant Clarke (1891-1931), Al Piantadosi (1884-1955)

Where Did You Get That Hat? (1888) w.m. Joseph J. Sullivan

Where Oh Where Has My Little Dog Gone see **Oh Where Oh Where Has My Little Dog Gone**

Where the Morning Glories Grow (1917) w. Gus Kahn (1886-1941), Raymond B. Egan (1890-1952) m. Richard A. Whiting (1891-1938)

Where the River Shannon Flows (1905) w.m. James J. Russell (? -1900 M)

While Strolling Through the Park One Day (The Fountain in the Park) (1884) w.m. Ed Haley (1862/63-1932) (Ed Haley is a pseudonym of Robert A. King). (F) Hollywood Revue, Sunbonnet Sue

Whip-Poor-Will (1920) w. Bud (B.G.) De Sylva (1895-1950) m. Jerome Kern (1885-1945). (M) Sally (F) Look for the Silver Lining

Whispering (1920) w.m. John Schonberger (1892-1983 A), Vincent Rose (1880-1944), Richard Coburn (1886-1952). (Richard Coburn is a pseudonym of Frank D. de Long). (F) Ziegfield Girl, Belles on Their Toes, The Eddy Duchin Story. *Some sources credit Malvin Schonberger as a composer of this song. Nothing is known about his birth and death dates.*

Whispering Hope (1868) w.m. Alice Hawthorne (1827-1902) (Alice Hawthorne is a pseudonym of Septimus Winner)

Whistler and His Dog, The (1905) m. Arthur Pryor (1870-1942). (F) The Emperor Waltz. This instrumental selection was often used in "Our Gang" comedies.

Who Threw the Overalls in Mrs. Murphy's Chowder (1898/99)
w.m. George L. Giefer

Wiegenlied (Lullaby) (1868) m. Johannes Brahms (1833-1897)

Wiener Blut (Vienna Life) (1873) Waltz. m. Johann Strauss, Jr. (1825-1899) (Op. 354)

Will You Love Me in December as You Do in May (1905) w. James J. Walker (1881-1946 A) m. Ernest R. Ball (1878-1927). (F) The Eddy Duchin Story (F) Beau James

Will You Remember (sweetheart) (1917) w. Rida Johnson Young (1869-1926) m. Sigmund Romberg (1887-1951). (M) Maytime (F) Maytime, Deep in My Heart

William Tell Overture (1829) From the opera, "William Tell." m. Gioacchino Rossini (1792-1868). Used as the basis for the "Lone Ranger Theme," also used in the silent movie era for chase scenes.

Wine, Women and Song (1869) Waltz. m. Johann Strauss, Jr. (1825-1899) (Op. 333)

(My) Wonderful One (1922) w. Dorothy Terriss (1890-1953) (Dorothy Terriss is a pseudonym of Theodora Morse) m. Paul Whiteman (1890-1967), Ferde Grofé (1892-1972). (F) Margie. *Adapted from a theme by Marshall Neilan. We have been unable to find any information on birth and death dates for Marshall Neilan, but since his theme predated the writing of this song, the song is in the Public Domain in the United States.*

World is Waiting for the Sunrise, The (1919) w. Eugene Lockhart (1891-1957 A) m. Ernest Seitz

Yaaka Hula Hickey Dula (1916) w. E. Ray Goetz (1886-1954), Joe Young (1889-1939) m. Pete Wendling (1888-1974 A). (M) Robinson Crusoe, Jr. (F) Applause

Yale Boola (Boola, Boola) (1901) Anonymous American. Based on "La Hoola Boola," (1898) by Robert (Bob) Cole (1869-1911) and Billy Johnson

Yankee Doodle (1700's) Traditional American

Yankee Doodle Boy (I Am the) (1904) w.m. George M. Cohan (1878-1942). (M) Little Johnny Jones, George M!, Dancin' (F) Little Johnny Jones, Yankee Doodle Dandy, The Seven Little Foys

Yellow Rose of Texas (1858) w.m. J. K. Traditional American. (F) Night Stage to Galveston. *The 1955 adaptation of this song, by Don George, is* **not** *Public Domain.*

You Ain't Heard Nothing Yet (1919) w. Al Jolson (1886-1950), Gus Kahn (1886-1941), m. Bud (B.G.) De Sylva (1895-1950)

You Belong to Me (1916) w. Harry B. Smith (1860-1936) m. Victor Herbert (1859-1924). (M) The Century Girl. *There are two other well-known songs by the same title. One is by Pee Wee King, Redd Stewart and Chilton Price; the other is by Carly Simon and Michael McDonald. These two other songs are* **not** *Public Domain.*

You Know and I Know (and we both understand) (1915) w. Schuyler Greene (1880-1927 A) m. Jerome Kern (1885-1945). (M) Nobody Home

You Made Me Love You (I didn't want to do it) (1913) w. Joseph McCarthy (1885-1943) m. James V. Monaco (1885-1945). Harry James' theme song. (F) The Jolson Story, Broadway Melody of 1938, Love Me or Leave Me, Jolson Sings Again

You Tell Her, I S-t-u-t-t-e-r (1922) w. William (Billy) Rose (1899-1966) m. Cliff Friend (1893-1974). (F) Millions in the Air

You Tell Me Your Dream (I had a dream, dear) (1908) w.m. Charles N. Daniels (1878-1943), Jay Blackton (1909-1994 A), Albert H. Brown, Seymour Rice

You'd Be Surprised (1919) w.m. Irving Berlin (1888-1989). (M) The Ziegfeld Follies 1919 (F) Blue Skies, There's No Business Like Show Business

You're a Grand Old Flag (1906) w.m. George M. Cohan (1878-1942). (M) George Washington Jr., George M! (F) Yankee Doodle Dandy

Zauberflöte, Die (The Magic Flute) (1791) Opera. w. E. Schikaneder (1751-1812) m. W.A. Mozart (1756-1791)

If you are selecting a song by looking through this category list, you must make sure to use it as written by the writers and composers of the Public Domain version of the song. Please refer back to the A to Z list for the names of those writers and composers.

Composers with four or more songs in the book are listed in a section by themselves along with their songs, directly following this category listing.

Blues Selections
Beale Street
Jazz Me Blues
Jelly Roll Blues
Joe Turner Blues
(I've Got the) Lovesick Blues
Limehouse Blues
Memphis Blues
St. Louis Blues
Sugar Blues
Wabash Blues
Wang Wang Blues, The

Children's Songs
A-Hunting We Will Go
A-Tisket A-Tasket
Alouette
Alphabet Song (A, b, c, d, etc.)
Are You Sleeping (Frère Jacques)
Au Clair de la Lune (Mon ami, Pierrot)
Baa, Baa, Black Sheep
Baby Bunting
Big Rock Candy Mountain
Billy Boy
Bingo
Ding Dong Bell
Evening Prayer (Now I Lay Me Down to Sleep—from the opera, "Hansel
    and Gretel")
Farmer in the Dell, The
Frère Jacques (Are You Sleeping)
Hey, Diddle Diddle
Hickory Dickory Dock
Hot Cross Buns

Humpty Dumpty
I Don't Want to Play in Your Yard
Jack and Jill
Jack Be Nimble
Jack Sprat
Limehouse Blues
Little Bo-Peep
Little Boy Blue
Little Jack Horner
Little Miss Muffet
Little Tommy Tucker
London Bridge
(I've Got the) Lovesick Blues
Lullaby (Brahms)
Mary Had a Little Lamb
Mistress Mary Quite Contrary
Mulberry Bush
Now I Lay Me Down to Sleep (Evening Prayer—from the opera, "Hansel
	and Gretel")
O (Ach) Du Lieber Augustin (Polly [Molly] Put the Kettle On; Did You Ever See a
	Lassie?)
Oh! Dear, What Can the Matter Be?
Oh Where, Oh Where Has My Little Dog Gone
Old King Cole
Old MacDonald Had a Farm
Parade of the Wooden Soldiers
Pease Porridge Hot
Peter Peter Pumpkin Eater
Polly (Molly) Put the Kettle On (O [Ach] Du Lieber Augustin; Did You Ever See a
	Lassie?)
Polly-Wolly-Doodle
Pop Goes the Weasel
Ring Around the (a) Rosie
Rock-A-Bye Baby
Row, Row, Row Your Boat
See Saw, Margery Daw
Sing a Song of Sixpence
Skip to My Lou
Sur le Pont d'Avignon
Sweet and Low
Teddy Bears' Picnic, The
Ten Little Indians (Injuns)
This Old Man
Three Blind Mice
Three Little Kittens

Toyland
Turkey in the Straw
Twinkle, Twinkle, Little Star
Where Oh Where Has My Little Dog Gone (see Oh Where, Oh Where Has My Little
    Dog Gone)
Yankee Doodle

Christmas Selections
Adeste Fideles (O Come All Ye Faithful)
Angels from the Realms of Glory
Angels We Have Heard on High
Ave Maria (Bach/Gounod)
Ave Maria (Schubert)
Away in a Manger
Boar's Head Carol, The
Cantique de Noël (O Holy Night)
Christmas Oratorio
Christmas Wishes
Coventry Carol, The (Lully, Lullay)
Deck the Halls
Dona Nobis Pacem
First Noël, The
God Rest Ye Merry Gentlemen
Good Christian Men, Rejoice
Good King Wenceslas
Hallelujah Chorus (Messiah)
Hark! The Herald Angels Sing
Here We Go/Come A-Caroling/A-Wassailing (Wassail Song)
Holly and the Ivy, The
I Heard the Bells on Christmas Day
I Saw Three Ships
Il Est Né Le Devin Enfant
It Came Upon a Midnight Clear
Jingle Bells
Jolly Old St. Nicholas
Joy to the World
Lully, Lullay (The Coventry Carol)
March of the Toys
Nutcracker Suite, The
O Come All Ye Faithful (Adeste Fideles)
O Come, O Come, Emmanuel
O Holy Night (Cantique de Noël)
O Little Town of Bethlehem
O Tännenbaum, O Tännenbaum

Patapan
Parade of the Wooden Soldiers
Silent Night
Toyland
Twelve Days of Christmas
Up on the Housetop
Wassail Song (Here We Go/Come A-Caroling/A-Wassailing)
We Three Kings of Orient Are
We Wish You a Merry Christmas
What Child is This?

Classical Selections

Ah! So Pure (from the opera, "Martha")
Aida (opera—Verdi)
Air for the G String
Also Sprach Zarathustra
Anvil Chorus (Verdi)
Apache Dance (Offenbach)
Artist's Life
Ave Maria (Bach/Gounod)
Ave Maria (Schubert)
Barcarolle (Offenbach)
Berceuse (from the opera, "Jocelyn")
Blue Danube, The
Bourrée (from "Water Music" - Handel)
Bourrée (from "Royal Fireworks Music" - Handel)
Brandenburg Concertos
Calvary
Can Can
Capriccio Espagnol
Capriccio Italien
Caprice Viennois
Carmen (opera—Bizet)
Chopsticks
Christmas Oratorio
Clair de Lune
Concerto for Piano
Coriolan Overture
Coronation March (Marche du Sacre, La)
Cosi Fan Tutte (opera—Mozart))
Creation, The (Haydn)
Dance of the Hours
Daphnis et Chloé (ballet)
Don Giovanni (opera—Mozart)

Drinking Song (Libiamo—from the opera,"La Traviata")
Du Und Du (from the operetta, "Die Fledermaus")
1812 Overture (Tchaikovsky)
Egmont Overture
Elijah
Emperor Waltz
España
Estudiantina
Evening Prayer (Now I Lay Me Down to Sleep—from the opera, "Hansel and
 Gretel")
Fantaisie-Impromptu (Chopin)
Finlandia (Sibelius)
Fledermaus, Die (operetta—Strauss)
Flight of the Bumblebee, The
Forza del Destino, La (opera—Verdi)
Four Seasons, The
Funeral March (Chopin)
Funeral March of a Marionette
Für Elise
Giselle (ballet)
Gold and Silver Waltz
Goldberg Variations
Golliwogg's Cake Walk
Götterdämmerung (opera—Wagner)
Habanera (from the opera, "Carmen")
Hallelujah Chorus (from the oratorio "Messiah")
Happy Farmer, The (The Merry Peasant)
Humoresque (Dvorák)
Hungarian Dance No. 5 (Brahms)
Hungarian Rhapsody No. 2
In the Hall of the Mountain King (Grieg)
Jesu, Joy of Man's Desiring
Jupiter Symphony
Kleine Nachtmusik, Eine (Mozart)
Largo (Dvorák)
Leonore Overture No. 3
Liebesfreud
Liebesleid
Liebestod
Liebestraum
Light Cavalry Overture
Lost Chord, The
Lullaby (Brahms)
Madama Butterfly (opera—Puccini)
Magic Flute, The (Die Zauberflöte) (opera—Mozart)

March (from the opera, "Tannhaüser")
March of the Dwarfs (Grieg)
Marche du Sacre, La (Coronation March)
Marche Slave
Melody in F
Mer, La
Merry Peasant, The (The Happy Farmer)
Merry Widow Waltz
Messiah
Minuet in G (Beethoven)
Minuet in G (Paderewski)
Minute Waltz (Chopin)
Moonlight Sonata (Beethoven)
Musetta's Waltz (from the opera, "La Bohème")
My Heart at Thy Sweet Voice
New World Symphony
Night on Bald Mountain
Nocturne Op. 9, No.2 (Chopin)
Now I Lay Me Down to Sleep (Evening Prayer—from the opera,
        "Hansel and Gretel")
Nozze di Figaro, Le (opera—Mozart)
Nutcracker Suite, The
Ode to Joy (Beethoven)
Otello (opera—Verdi)
Pachelbel's Canon
Peer Gynt
Piano Concerto No. 1 (Tchaikovsky)
Poet and Peasant Overture
Polonaise in A-flat (Chopin)
Polonaise Militaire (Chopin)
Polovetsian Dances
Pomp and Circumstance
Prelude (Chopin)
Prince of Denmark's March (Clarke)
Rheingold, Das (opera—Wagner)
Reverie (Debussy)
Ride of the Valkyries
Rigoletto (opera—Verdi)
Ring des Nibelungen, Der (Wagner)
Romance
Royal Fireworks Music (Handel)
Scheherazade
Seasons, The
Seigfried (opera—Wagner)
Skaters' Waltz

Slavonic Dances
Sleeping Beauty (ballet)
Sorcerer's Apprentice, The
Spring Song (Mendelssohn)
St. John Passion
St. Matthew Passion
Swan Lake (ballet)
Symphony No. 1 (Brahms)
Symphony No. 3 "Eroica" (Beethoven)
Symphony No. 5 (Beethoven)
Symphony No. 6 "Pastorale" (Beethoven)
Symphony No. 9 "Choral" (Beethoven)
Tales from the Vienna Woods
To a Wild Rose
Toreador Song (from the opera, "Carmen")
Traümerei (Schumann)
Traviata, La (opera—Verdi)
Tristan und Isolde (opera—Wagner)
Triumphal March (from the opera, "Aida")
Trout Quintet
Trumpet Voluntary ("Purcell" - see listing for "Prince of Denmark's March")
Un Bel Di (from the opera, "Madama Butterfly")
Unfinished Symphony (Schubert)
Valse Bleue
Valse, La
Vesti la Giubba (from the opera, "I Pagliacci")
Vienna Life (Wiener Blut)
Vissi d'Arte (from the opera, "Tosca")
Walküre, Die (opera—Wagner)
Waltz (from the ballet, "Coppelia")
Waltz (from the opera, "Romeo et Juliette")
Waltz of the Flowers (from "The Nutcracker Suite")
Water Music (Handel)
Waves of the Danube
Wedding March (Here comes the bride) (Wagner)
Wedding March (Recessional) (Mendelssohn)
Well-Tempered Clavier,The (Books I & II)
Wiegenlied (Lullaby) (Brahms)
Wiener Blut (Vienna Life)
William Tell Overture (Rossini)
Wine, Women and Song
Zauberflöte, Die (The Magic Flute)

Folksongs

Alouette
Annie Laurie
Are You Sleeping (Frère Jacques)
Arkansas Traveler, The
Big Rock Candy Mountain
Billy Boy
Bingo
Blow the Man Down
Blue Tail Fly, The (Jimmy Crack Corn)
Bobby Shafto
Casey Jones
Chicken Reel, The
Clementine (Oh, My Darling Clementine)
Cockles and Mussels ([Sweet] Molly Malone)
Comin' Thro' the Rye (If a body meet a body)
Cotton Gin Reel
Cowboy's Lament, The (Streets of Laredo)
Did You Ever See a Lassie? (O [Ach] Du Lieber Augustin; Polly [Molly] Put the Kettle
    On)
Danny Boy
Dove, The (La Paloma)
Erie Canal (Fifteen Miles [Years] on the Erie Canal; Low Bridge!
    Everybody Down)
Frère Jacques (Are You Sleeping)
Git Along Little Dogies (Whoopee ti yi yo)
Greensleeves
Home on the Range
I've Been Working on the Railroad (Someone's in the kitchen with Dinah)
Jarabe Tapatio (Mexican Hat Dance)
Jimmy Crack Corn (The Blue Tail Fly)
John Brown's Body
Loch Lomond (O! Ye'll Take the High Road)
Londonderry Air
Low Bridge! Everybody Down (Erie Canal; Fifteen Miles [Years] on the
    Erie Canal)
Mexican Hat Dance (Jarabe Tapatio)
Molly Malone [Sweet] (Cockles and Mussels)
O (Ach) Du Lieber Augustin (Polly [Molly] Put the Kettle On; Did You Ever See
    a Lassie?)
Oh, My Darling Clementine (Clementine)
Old Folks at Home (Way Down Upon the Swanee River)
Old Grey Mare
On Top of Old Smokey
Otchi Tchorniya (Translated as Dark Eyes)

Paloma, La (The Dove)
Polly [Molly] Put the Kettle On (O [Ach] Du Lieber Augustin; Did You Ever See
     a Lassie?)
Polly-Wolly-Doodle
Red River Valley, The
'Round Her Neck She Wears (Wore) a Yellow (Yeller) Ribbon (She Wore a Yellow
     Ribbon)
Sailor's Hornpipe
Santa Lucia
Scarborough Fair
Shenandoah
Skip to My Lou
Song of the Volga Boatmen
Streets of Laredo (The Cowboy's Lament)
Sweet Betsy from Pike
Sweet Molly Malone (Cockles and Mussels)
Turkey in the Straw
Wait for the Wagon
Way Down Upon the Swanee River (Old Folks at Home)

Inspirational Songs
Abide with Me (Fast falls the eventide)
All Through the Night
Amazing Grace
Battle Hymn of the Republic (Glory, glory hallelujah)
Blest Be the Tie That Binds
Calvary
Come, Thou Almighty King
Come Unto Me
Deep River
Down By the Riverside (Ain't gwine to study war no more)
Elijah
Faith of Our Fathers
Feste Burg, Ein' (A Mighty Fortress is Our God)
Go Down Moses
Holy, Holy, Holy, Lord God Almighty
In the Garden
In the Great Somewhere
Lead, Kindly Light
Let Us Break Bread Together
Lift Every Voice and Sing
Little David Play on Your Harp
Mighty Fortress is Our God, A (Feste Burg, Ein')
My Mother's Rosary

Nearer, My God, to Thee
Nobody Knows the Trouble I've Seen
Now I Lay Me Down to Sleep
Now the Day is Over
O God, Our Help in Ages Past
Oh, Didn't It Rain
Old Hundred(th) Doxology (Praise God from Whom All Blessings Flow)
Old Rugged Cross, The
Onward, Christian Soldiers
Praise God from Whom All Blessings Flow (Old Hundred[th] Doxology)
Prayer of Thanksgiving (We Gather Together)
Rock of Ages
Rosary, The
Rose of Sharon, The
Seasons, The
St. John Passion
St. Matthew Passion
Steal Away
'Tis Me Oh Lord, Standin' in de Need of Pray'r
We Gather Together (Prayer of Thanksgiving)
What a Friend We Have in Jesus

International Favorites

All Through the Night
Aloha Oe
Along the Rocky Road to Dublin
Alouette
Annie Laurie
Are You Sleeping (Frère Jacques)
Au Clair de la Lune (Mon ami, Pierrot)
Auf Wiedersehen
Blue Bell of Scotland, The
Britannia, the Gem of the Ocean
Campbells Are Coming, The
Choclo, El
Ciribiribin
Cockles and Mussels ([Sweet] Molly Malone)
Comin' Thro' the Rye (If a body meet a body)
Danny Boy
Did You Ever See a Lassie? (O [Ach] Du Lieber Augustin; Polly [Molly] Put the Kettle On)
Dove, The (La Paloma)
Drink to Me Only with Thine Eyes
Flow Gently, Sweet Afton

Frère Jacques (Are You Sleeping)
Funiculì, Funiculà
Gaudeamus Igitur
God Save the King
I Love a Lassie (Ma Scotch Bluebell)
In the Gloaming
Ireland is Ireland to Me
Ireland Must Be Heaven, for My Mother Came from There
Irish Washerwoman, The
Jarabe Tapatio (Mexican Hat Dance)
Kerry Dance (Oh the days of the Kerry dancing)
Little Annie Rooney
Little Bit of Heaven, Sure They Call It Ireland, A
Loch Lomond (Oh! Ye'll Take the High Road)
Londonderry Air
MacNamara's Band
Mexican Hat Dance (Jarabe Tapatio)
Mother Machree
My Bonnie Lies Over the Ocean
My Wild Irish Rose
O (Ach) Du Lieber Augustin (Polly [Molly] Put the Kettle On; Did You Ever See
        a Lassie?)
'O Sole Mio
On the Road to Mandalay
Otchi Tchorniya (Translated as Dark Eyes)
Paloma, La (The Dove)
Polly (Molly) Put the Kettle On (O [Ach] Du Lieber Augustin; Did You Ever See a
        Lassie?)
Roamin' in the Gloamin'
Rule Britannia
Santa Lucia
Song of the Volga Boatmen
Sur le Pont d'Avignon
Sweet Molly Malone (Cockles and Mussels)
That Old Irish Mother of Mine
That Tumble-Down Shack in Athlone
That's an Irish Lullaby (Too-Ra-Loo-Ra-Loo-Ral, That's an Irish Lullaby)
Torna a Surriento!
Vive la Compagnie
Wearin' of the Green
When Irish Eyes Are Smiling
Where the River Shannon Flows
Who Threw the Overalls in Mrs. Murphy's Chowder

Love Songs

Aba Daba Honeymoon, The
After the Ball
Ah! Sweet Mystery of Life
Annie Laurie
Auf Wiedersehen
Be My Little Baby Bumble Bee
Beautiful Dreamer
Because
Because You're You
Believe Me If All Those Endearing Young Charms
Bicycle Built for Two, A (Daisy Bell)
Clementine (Oh, My Darling Clementine)
Cuddle Up a Little Closer, Lovey Mine
Darling Nelly Gray
Do It Some More (and more and more)
Down By the Old Mill Stream
Drink to Me Only with Thine Eyes
Fascination
For Me and My Gal
Fountain in the Park, The (While Strolling Through the Park One Day)
Give Me the Moonlight, Give Me the Girl
Greensleeves
Gypsy Love Song (Slumber On)
Hello, Ma Baby
How'd You Like to Spoon with Me?
I Love a Lassie
I Love You Truly
I Might Be Your Once-In-A-While
I Want a Girl (Just Like the Girl That Married Dear Old Dad)
I Wonder Who's Kissing Her Now
I'd Love to Live in Loveland (With a girl like you)
Ida, Sweet as Apple Cider
If I Had My Way
If You Were the Only Girl in the World
I'll Take You Home Again, Kathleen
I'm Falling in Love with Someone
I'm Sorry I Made You Cry
It's Delightful to Be Married
Jeannie with the Light Brown Hair
Just a Song at Twilight (Love's Old Sweet Song)
Kiss in the Dark, A
L'Amour-Toujours-L'Amour (Love Everlasting)
Let Me Call You Sweetheart
Little Love, a Little Kiss, A

Loads of Lovely Love
Love is the Best of All
Love Me and the World is Mine
Love's Old Sweet Song (Just a Song at Twilight)
(I've Got the) Lovesick Blues
Meet Me Tonight in Dreamland
Moonlight Bay (On Moonlight Bay)
My Bonnie Lies Over the Ocean
My Buddy
My Gal Sal
My Man
My Melancholy Baby
My Wife Won't Let Me (Waiting at the Church)
My Wild Irish Rose
Nelly Bly
Oh! By Jingo, Oh! By Gee, You're the Only Girl for Me
Oh Johnny, Oh Johnny, Oh
Oh, My Darling Clementine (Clementine)
Oh! Susanna
Oh! What a Pal Was Mary
Oh, You Beautiful Doll
Peg o' My Heart
Put On Your Old Grey Bonnet
Put Your Arms Around Me, Honey (Hold me tight)
Red River Valley, The
Roamin' in the Gloamin'
Shine On, Harvest Moon
Silver Threads Among the Gold
Smile the While You Kiss Me Sad Adieu (Till We Meet Again)
Snookey Ookums
Song of Love
Sweet Adeline
Sweethearts
Thine Alone
Wait Till the Sun Shines, Nellie
Waiting at the Church (My Wife Won't Let Me)
When Irish Eyes Are Smiling
When You and I Were Young, Maggie
When You Were Sweet Sixteen
When You Wore a Tulip (And I wore a big red rose)
When You're in Love with Someone Who is Not in Love with You
While Strolling Through the Park One Day (The Fountain in the Park)
Will You Love Me in December as You Do in May
Will You Remember (sweetheart)
(My) Wonderful One

You Belong to Me
You Know and I Know (And we both understand)
You Made Me Love You (I didn't want to do it)
You Tell Me Your Dream (I had a dream, dear)

Marches

American Patrol
Caissons Go Rolling Along, The
Capitan, El (Sousa)
Colonel Bogey March
Fort Sumpter March
Gladiator, The (Sousa)
Gladiator's Entry, The
Hail to the Chief
Hands Across the Sea (Sousa)
King Cotton (Sousa)
Manhattan Beach March (Sousa)
March (from the opera, "Tannhaüser")
March of the Dwarfs (Grieg)
March of the Toys
Marching Through Georgia (Civil War)
Marines' Hymn (From the halls of Montezuma)
Marseillaise, La
National Emblem March (When/and the monkey wrapped his tail around the flagpole)
        (Performed at circuses)
New York Hippodrome March (Sousa)
Semper Fidelis (Sousa)
Stars and Stripes Forever (Sousa)
Thunderer, The (Sousa)
Washington Post March (Sousa)

Patriotic Songs (includes songs associated with wars)

America (My country 'tis of thee)
America the Beautiful
American Patrol
Anchors Aweigh
Battle Hymn of the Republic (Glory, glory hallelujah)
Battle Cry of Freedom
Bonnie Blue Flag, The
Caissons Go Rolling Along, The
Colonel Bogey March
Dixie
Fort Sumpter March

Good-Bye Broadway, Hello, France!
Hail to the Chief
It's a Long, Long Way to Tipperary
Johnny Get Your Gun
Keep the Home-Fires Burning (Till the boys come home)
Manhattan Beach March
Marching Through Georgia
Marines' Hymn (From the halls of Montezuma)
Oh! How I Hate to Get Up in the Morning
Over There
Pack Up Your Troubles in Your Old Kit-Bag
Semper Fidelis (Sousa)
Star Spangled Banner, The
Stars and Stripes Forever
Taps
Tenting on the Old Camp Ground
Tramp, Tramp, Tramp (The boys are marching)
We're Going Over
When Johnny Comes Marching Home
Yankee Doodle
Yankee Doodle Boy (I Am the)
You're a Grand Old Flag

Place Names in Songs
Along the Rocky Road to Dublin
America (My country 'tis of thee)
America the Beautiful
Arkansas Traveler, The
Avalon
Beale Street
Beautiful Ohio
Bimini Bay
Blue Bell of Scotland, The
Bowery, The
Britannia, the Gem of the Ocean
Broadway Rose
By the Waters of Minnetonka
Carolina in the Morning
Carry Me Back to Old Virginny
Chicago (That Toddling Town)
Chinatown, My Chinatown
Dixie
Erie Canal (Fifteen Miles [Years] on the Erie Canal; Low Bridge! Everybody Down)
Everything is Peaches Down in Georgia

Finlandia
Fort Sumpter March
Give My Regards to Broadway
Good-Bye Broadway, Hello, France!
Hello, Frisco, Hello
How You ('Ya) Going to Keep 'Em Down on the Farm After They've Seen Paree?
How's Every Little Thing in Dixie
I Want to Go Back to Michigan, Down on the Farm
I'm All Bound 'Round with the Mason-Dixon Line
In Old New York (The Streets of New York)
Indiana (Back Home Again in)
Ireland is Ireland to Me
Ireland Must Be Heaven, for My Mother Came from There
It's a Long, Long Way to Tipperary
It's Tulip Time in Holland
Jarabe Taptio (Mexican Hat Dance)
Kentucky Babe (Sleep, Kentucky Babe)
Limehouse Blues
Little Bit of Heaven, Sure They Call It Ireland, A
Loch Lomond (Oh! Ye'll Take the High Road)
London Bridge
Londonderry Air
Low Bridge! Everybody Down (Erie Canal; Fifteen Miles [Years] on the Erie Canal)
Manhattan Beach March
Marching Through Georgia
Maryland, My Maryland
Meet Me in St. Louis, Louis
Memphis Blues, The
Mexican Hat Dance (Jarabe Tapatio)
M-I-S-S-I-S-S-I-P-P-I
Missouri Waltz, The (Hush-a-bye, Ma Baby)
My Best Girl's a New Yorker (Corker)
My Old Kentucky Home
New York Hippodrome March
On the Beach at Waikiki
On Wisconsin
Rock-a-Bye Your Baby with a Dixie Melody
Rose of the Rio Grande
Rose of Washington Square
Roses of Picardy
Rule Britannia
Shenandoah (Across the Wide Missouri)
Sidewalks of New York, The (East Side, West Side)
Song of the Volga Boatmen
St. Louis Blues

Streets of Laredo (The Cowboy's Lament)
Streets of New York, The (In Old New York)
That Old Irish Mother of Mine
That Tumble-Down Shack in Athlone
Torna a Surriento!
Vienna Life (Wiener Blut)
Wabash Blues
Washington Post March
Way Down Yonder in New Orleans
When It's Apple Blossom Time in Normandy
When the/That Midnight Choo-Choo Leaves for Alabam'
Where the River Shannon Flows
Yellow Rose of Texas

Popular Songs

Aba Daba Honeymoon, The
After the Ball
After You've Gone
Ah! Sweet Mystery of Life
Ain't We Got Fun
Alexander's Ragtime Band
(In My Sweet Little) Alice Blue Gown
All By Myself
April Showers
And the Green Grass Grew All Around
Asleep in the Deep
Auld Lang Syne
Avalon
Babes in the Wood
Baby Shoes
Baby Won't You Please Come Home
(Back Home Again in) Indiana
Ballin' the Jack
Band Played On, The (Casey would waltz with the strawberry blonde)
Be My Little Baby Bumble Bee
Beale Street
Beautiful Dreamer
Beautiful Isle of Somewhere
Beautiful Ohio
Because
Because You're You
Bedelia
Believe Me If All Those Endearing Young Charms
Bells of St. Mary's, The

Bicycle Built for Two, A (Daisy Bell)
Bill Bailey, Won't You Please Come Home?
Bimini Bay
Bird in a Gilded Cage, A
Boola, Boola (Yale Boola)
Bowery, The
Breeze from Alabama, A
Britannia (Columbia), the Gem of the Ocean
Broadway Rose
By the Beautiful Sea
By the Light of the Silvery Moon
By the Waters of Minnetonka
Camptown Races, De
Can Can
Carolina in the Morning
Carry Me Back to Old Virginny
Casey Jones
Chicago (That Toddling Town)
Chinatown, My Chinatown
Choclo, El
Chopsticks
Chrysanthemum, The
Ciribiribin
Clementine (Oh, My Darling Clementine)
Colonel Bogey March
Columbia (Brittania), the Gem of the Ocean
Come, Josephine, in My Flying Machine
Come to the Fair
Cuddle Up a Little Closer, Lovey Mine
Daddy Long Legs
Daddy's Little Girl
Daisy Bell (A Bicycle Built for Two)
Danny Boy
Dardanella
Daring Young Man, The (On the Flying Trapeze)
Darktown Strutters' Ball, The
Darling Nelly Gray
Daughter of Rosie O'Grady, The
Dear Little Boy of Mine
Dear Old Pal of Mine
Do It Again
Do It Some More (and more and more)
Don't Go in the Lion's Cage Tonight
Down Among the Sheltering Palms
Down By the Old Mill Stream

Down in Honky Tonky Town
Drink to Me Only with Thine Eyes
East Side, West Side (The Sidewalks of New York)
Easy Winners, The
Entertainer, The
Every Day is Ladies' Day with Me
Every Little Movement (Has a meaning all its own)
Everybody's Doin' It Now
Everything is Peaches Down in Georgia
Flirtation Waltz
Flow Gently, Sweet Afton
Flying Trapeze, The (The Daring Young Man on the)
For He's a Jolly Good Fellow
For Me and My Gal
Fountain in the Park, The (While Strolling Through the Park One Day)
From the Land of the Sky-Blue Water
Funiculì, Finiculà
Giannina Mia
Girl I Left Behind Me, The (used at West Point)
Girl on the Magazine Cover
Give Me the Moonlight, Give Me the Girl
Give My Regards to Broadway
Glow-Worm, The
Golden Slippers (Oh Dem Golden Slippers)
Good Man is Hard to Find, A
Good Night Ladies
Goodbye, Girls, I'm Through
Goodbye, Good Luck, God Bless You
Goodbye, My Lady Love
Grandfather's Clock
Greensleeves
Gypsy Love Song (Slumber On)
Hail, Hail, the Gang's All Here
Hand Me Down My Walking Cane
Harrigan
Has Anybody Here Seen Kelly?
Have a Heart
Hearts and Flowers
Hello, Frisco, Hello
Hello, Ma Baby
He's a Devil in His Own Home Town
Hindustan
Hold That Tiger! (Tiger Rag)
Home on the Range (Oh, give me a home where the buffalo roam)
Home Sweet Home (Be It Ever So Humble)

Hootchy Kootchy Dance (Streets of Cairo, The) (Oh they don't wear pants in the
    Southern part of France)
Hot Time in the Old Town Tonight (There'll Be a)
How You ('Ya) Going to Keep 'Em Down on the Farm After They've Seen Paree?
How'd You Like to Spoon with Me?
How's Every Little Thing in Dixie
I Ain't Got Nobody
I Didn't Raise My Boy to Be a Soldier
I Don't Care
I Don't Want to Play in Your Yard
I Love a Lassie
I Love a Piano
I Love You Truly
I Might Be Your Once-In-A-While
I Used to Love You, But It's All Over Now
I Want a Girl (Just Like the Girl That Married Dear Old Dad)
I Want to Go Back to Michigan, Down on the Farm
I Wish I Could Shimmy (Shemmi) Like My Sister Kate
I Wish I Had a Girl
I Wonder Who's Kissing Her Now
I'd Love to Live in Loveland (With a girl like you)
Ida, Sweet as Apple Cider
If I Had My Way
If I Were on the Stage (Kiss Me Again)
If You Don't Want My Peaches, You'd Better Stop Shaking My Tree
If You Had All the World and Its Gold
If You Were the Only Girl in the World
I'll Be With You in Apple Blossom Time
I'll Build a Stairway to Paradise
I'll Take You Home Again, Kathleen
I'm All Bound 'Round with the Mason-Dixon Line
I'm Always Chasing Rainbows
I'm Falling in Love with Someone
I'm Forever Blowing Bubbles
I'm Just Wild About Harry
I'm Nobody's Baby
I'm Sorry I Made You Cry
In a Monastery Garden
In My Merry Oldsmobile
(In My Sweet Little) Alice Blue Gown
In Old New York (The Streets of New York)
In the Evening by the Moonlight
In the Good Old Summertime
In the Shade of the Old Apple Tree
In the Sweet Bye and Bye

Indiana (Back Home Again in)
Indianola
Italian Street Song
It's a Long, Long Way to Tipperary
It's Delightful to Be Married
It's Tulip Time in Holland
I've Been Working on the Railroad (Someone's in the kitchen with Dinah)
I've Got Rings on My Fingers
I've Got the Time—I've Got the Place, but It's Hard to Find the Girl
Ja-Da, Ja-Da, Ja-Da Jing-Jing-Jing
Japanese Sandman, The
Jazz Me Blues
Jeannie with the Light Brown Hair
Jelly Roll Blues
Joe Turner Blues
Johnny Get Your Gun
Just a Song at Twilight (Love's Old Sweet Song)
Just A-Wearyin' for You
Katinka
Keep the Home-Fires Burning (Till the boys come home)
Kentucky Babe (Sleep, Kentucky Babe)
Kiss in the Dark, A
Kiss Me Again (If I Were on the Stage)
Kitten on the Keys
K-K-K-Katy
L'Amour-Tourjours-L'Amour (Love Everlasting)
Let Me Call You Sweetheart
Let the Rest of the World Go By
Li'l Liza Jane
Lily of the Valley
Limehouse Blues
Listen to the Mocking Bird
Little Bit of Heaven, Sure They Call It Ireland, A
Little Brown Jug
Little Grey Home in the West
Little Love, a Little Kiss, A
Little Mother of Mine
Little Sir Echo
Loads of Lovely Love
Londonderry Air
Long, Long Ago
Look for the Silver Lining
Love is the Best of All
Love Me and the World is Mine
Love Nest, The

(I've Got the) Lovesick Blues
Love's Old Sweet Song (Just a Song at Twilight)
Ma! He's Making Eyes at Me
MacNamara's Band
Mammy O'Mine
Man on the Flying Trapeze, The (The Daring Young Man)
Mandy
Maple Leaf Rag
March of the Toys
Margie
Mary's a Grand Old Name
Meet Me In St. Louis, Louis
Meet Me Tonight in Dreamiand
Memories
Memphis Blues, The
Mighty Lak' a Rose
M-I-S-S-I-S-S-I-P-P-I
Missouri Waltz, The (Hush-a-bye, Ma Baby)
Mister Gallagher and Mister Shean
Moonbeams
Moonlight Bay (On Moonlight Bay)
M-O-T-H-E-R (A Word That Means the World to Me)
My Best Girl's a New Yorker (Corker)
My Bonnie Lies Over the Ocean
My Buddy
My Gal Sal
My Heart at Thy Sweet Voice
My Hero
My Little Girl
My Mammy
My Man
My Melancholy Baby
My Old Kentucky Home
My Pony Boy
My Sweetheart's the Man on the Moon
My Wife Won't Let Me (Waiting at the Church)
My Wild Irish Rose
National Emblem March (When/and the monkey wrapped his tail around
        the flagpole) (Performed at circuses)
Neapolitan Love Song
Nelly Was a Lady
Ninety-Nine Bottles of Beer on the Wall
Oceana Roll, The
Oh! By Jingo, Oh! By Gee, You're the Only Girl for Me
Oh! Dear, What Can the Matter Be?

Oh Dem Golden Slippers (Golden Slippers)
Oh! How I Hate to Get Up in the Morning
Oh! How She Could Yacki, Hacki, Wicki, Wacki, Woo
Oh Johnny, Oh Johnny, Oh
Oh, My Darling Clementine (Clementine)
Oh Promise Me
Oh! Susanna
Oh They Don't Wear Pants in the Southern Part of France (Hootchy Kootchy Dance)
        (Streets of Cairo, The)
Oh! What a Pal Was Mary
Oh Where, Oh Where Has My Little Dog Gone
Oh, You Beautiful Doll
Old Black Joe
Old Dan Tucker
Old-Fashioned Garden
Old-Fashioned Wife, An
Old Folks at Home (Way Down Upon the Swanee River)
Old Grey Mare
Old Oaken Bucket, The
On a Sunday Afternoon
On the Banks of the Wabash Far Away
On the Beach at Waikiki
On the 5:15
On the Road to Mandalay
On Wisconsin
Otchi Tchorniya (Translated as Dark Eyes)
Out Where the West Begins
Over There
Pack Up Your Troubles in Your Old Kit-Bag
Palm Leaf Rag
Peg o' My Heart
Perfect Day, A
Polly-Wolly-Doodle
Poor Butterfly
Pop Goes the Weasel
Pretty Baby
Pretty Girl is Like a Melody, A
Put On Your Old Grey Bonnet
Put Your Arms Around Me, Honey (Hold me tight)
Ragging the Scale
Ragtime Cowboy Joe
Red River Valley, The
Reflection Rag
Roamin' in the Gloamin'
Rock-a-Bye Baby

Rock-a-Bye Your Baby with a Dixie Melody
Rocked in the Cradle of the Deep
Rose of the Rio Grande
Rose of Washington Square
Roses of Picardy
Row, Row, Row (And then he'd)
Row, Row, Row Your Boat
Runnin' Wild
Sailing (Sailing, sailing over the bounding main)
Sally
Santa Lucia
Say It with Music
Scarborough Fair
School Days
Searchlight Rag
Second Hand Rose
She is More to Be Pitied Than Censured
Sheik of Araby, The
Shine On, Harvest Moon
Shoo Fly, Don't Bother Me
Shuffle Along
Sidewalks of New York, The (East Side, West Side)
Silver Sails
Silver Threads Among the Gold
Simple Melody
Sipping Cider Thru' A Straw
Smile the While You Kiss Me Sad Adieu (Till We Meet Again)
Smiles (There are smiles that make us happy)
Smilin' Through
Snookey Ookums
Solace
So Long Oo-Long, How Long You Gonna Be Gone?
Some of These Days
Some Sunday Morning
Somebody Stole My Gal
Sometime
Somewhere a Voice is Calling
Song of Love
Song of Songs, The
Songs My Mother Taught Me
Souvenirs
Spanish Moss
Spring is Everywhere
St. Louis Blues
Steamboat Bill

Streets of Cairo, The (Hootchy Kootchy Dance) (Oh they don't wear pants in the southern part of France)
Streets of New York, The (In Old New York)
Stumbling
Sunbonnet Sue
Sunshine of Your Smile, The
Swanee
Sweet Adeline
Sweet and Low
Sweet Betsy from Pike
Sweet Little Buttercup
Sweet Rosie O'Grady
Sweetheart of Sigma Chi, The
Sweethearts
Sycamore, The
Sylvia
Sympathy
Ta-Ra-Ra Boom-De-Ay
Take Me Out to the Ball Game
Teddy Bears' Picnic, The
That Old Irish Mother of Mine
That Tumble-Down Shack in Athlone
That Worlderful Mother of Mine
That's an Irish Lullaby (Too-Ra-Loo-Ra-Loo-Ral, That's an Irish Lullaby)
There is a Tavern in the Town
There'll Be a Hot Time in the Old Town Tonight
There'll Be Some Changes Made
There's a Broken Heart for Every Light on Broadway
There's a Long, Long Trail
There's a Quaker Down in Quaker Town
They Didn't Believe Me
They Go Wild Simply Wild Over Me
Thine Alone
Three O'Clock in the Morning
Throw Me a Rose
Tiger Rag (Hold That Tiger!)
Till the Clouds Roll By
Till We Meet Again (Smile the While You Kiss Me Sad Adieu)
'Tis the Last Rose of Summer
To a Wild Rose
Toot, Toot, Tootsie (Goo' Bye)
Torna a Surriento!
Toyland
Trail of the Lonesome Pine, The
Tramp! Tramp! Tramp! (Along the highway)

Tramp, Tramp, Tramp (The boys are marching)
Trees
Turkey in the Straw
Twelfth Street Rag
Under the Bamboo Tree
Valse Tzigane
Wabash Blues
Wait for the Wagon
Wait Till the Cows Come Home
Wait Till the Sun Shines, Nellie
Waiting at the Church (My Wife Won't Let Me)
Waiting for the Robert E. Lee
Waltz Me Around Again Willie—'Round 'Round 'Round
Wang Wang Blues, The
Way Down Upon the Swanee River (Old Folks at Home)
Way Down Yonder in New Orleans
Weeping Willow
What Do You Want to Make Those Eyes at Me For
When Hearts Are Young
When I Leave the World Behind
When Irish Eyes Are Smiling
When It's Apple Blossom Time in Normandy
When Johnny Comes Marching Home
When My Baby Smiles at Me
When the/That Midnight Choo-Choo Leaves For Alabam'
When You and I Were Young, Maggie
When You Were Sweet Sixteen
When You Wore a Tulip (And I wore a big red rose)
When You're a Long, Long Way from Home
When You're Away (dear)
When You're in Love with Someone Who is Not in Love with You
Where Did You Get That Hat?
Where the Morning Glories Grow
While Strolling Through the Park One Day (The Fountain in the Park)
Whip-Poor-Will
Whispering
Whispering Hope
Whistler and His Dog, The
Who Threw the Overalls in Mrs. Murphy's Chowder
Will You Love Me in December as You Do in May
Will You Remember (sweetheart)
(My) Wonderful One
World is Waiting for the Sunrise, The
Yaaka Hula Hickey Dula
Yale Boola (Boola, Boola)

Yankee Doodle
Yankee Doodle Boy, (I Am the)
Yellow Rose of Texas
You Ain't Heard Nothing Yet
You Belong to Me
You Know and I Know (And we both understand)
You Made Me Love You (I didn't want to do it)
You Tell Her, I S-t-u-t-t-e-r
You Tell Me Your Dream (I had a dream, dear)
You'd Be Surprised
You're a Grand Old Flag

Silent Film Era Songs

Hearts and Flowers (used in scenes where the villain demands payment of the
      mortgage "or else")
Please Go 'Way and Let Me Sleep (used in scenes where someone desperately
      needing help tries frantically to wake someone)
William Tell Overture (used in chase scenes)

Special Occasion Songs (birthday, graduation, wedding, etc.)

Anchors Aweigh
Assembly (Bugle Call) (There's a monkey in the grass)
Auld Lang Syne
For He's a Jolly Good Fellow
Funeral March (Chopin)
God Save the King
Good Night Ladies
Hail to the Chief
Marines' Hymn (From the halls of Montezuma)
Marseillaise, La
M-O-T-H-E-R (A Word That Means the World to Me)
National Emblem March (When/and the monkey wrapped his tail around the flagpole)
      (Performed at circuses)
Pomp and Circumstance (used at graduations)
Prayer of Thanksgiving (We Gather Together)
Reveille
Rule Britannia
Star Spangled Banner, The
Taps
Wedding March (Here comes the bride) (Wagner)
Wedding March (Recessional) (Mendelssohn)
When You Were Sweet Sixteen
Yale Boola (Boola, Boola)

Spirituals
Come Unto Me
Deep River
Down By the Riverside (Ain't gwine to study war no more)
Go Down Moses
In the Great Somewhere
Joshua Fit de Battle of Jericho
Let Us Break Bread Together
Little David Play on Your Harp
Nobody Knows the Trouble I've Seen
Oh, Didn't It Rain
Sometimes I Feel Like a Motherless Child
Steal Away
Swing Low, Sweet Chariot
'Tis Me Oh Lord, Standin' in de Need of Pray'r
What a Friend We Have in Jesus
When the Saints Go Marching In

Tangos
Choclo, El

Waltzes
Artist's Life
Blue Danube, The
Danube Waves (Waves of the Danube)
Du und Du (from the operetta, "Die Fledermaus")
Emperor Waltz
Flirtation Waltz
Gold and Silver Waltz
Merry Widow Waltz, The (I Love You So)
Minute Waltz
Musetta's Waltz (from the opera, "La Bohème")
Skaters' Waltz
Tales from the Vienna Woods
Valse Bleue
Valse Tzigane
Vienna Life (Wiener Blut)
Waltz of the Flowers (from "The Nutcracker Suite")
Waltz (from the ballet, "Coppelia")
Waltz (from the opera, "Romeo et Juliette")
Waves of the Danube (Danube Waves)
Wine, Women and Song

PROPERTY OF EL CAMINO COLLEGE
MUSIC LIBRARY

Composers with four or more songs in the Mini-Encyclopedia
There are many lesser-known selections in the Public Domain by these composers. If you'd like a longer list, please get in touch with us.

J. S. Bach Selections
Air for the G String
Ave Maria
Brandenburg Concertos
Christmas Oratorio
Goldberg Variations
Jesu, Joy of Man's Desiring
St. John Passion
St. Matthew Passion
Well-Tempered Clavier, The

Ernest R. Ball Songs
Dear Little Boy of Mine
Goodbye, Good Luck, God Bless You
Ireland Is Ireland to Me
Let the Rest of the World Go By
Little Bit of Heaven, Sure They Call It Ireland, A
Love Me and the World Is Mine
Mother Machree
When Irish Eyes Are Smiling
Will You Love Me in December As You Do in May

Ludwig van Beethoven Selections
Coriolan Overture
Egmont Overture
Für Elise
Leonore Overture No. 3
Minuet in G
Moonlight Sonata
Ode to Joy
Symphony No.3 ("Eroica")
Symphony No.5
Symphony No.6 ("Pastorale")
Symphony No.9 ("Choral")

Irving Berlin Songs
Alexander's Ragtime Band
All By Myself
Do It Again
Everybody's Doin' It Now
Girl on the Magazine Cover
He's a Devil in His Own Home Town
I Love a Piano
I Want to Go Back to Michigan, Down on the Farm
If You Don't Want My Peaches, You'd Better Stop Shaking My Tree
Mandy
Oh! How I Hate to Get Up in the Morning
Pretty Girl is Like a Melody, A
Say It with Music
Simple Melody
Snookey Ookums
When I Leave the World Behind
When the/That Midnight Choo-Choo Leaves for Alabam'
You'd Be Surprised

James A. Bland Songs
Carry Me Back to Old Virginny
Golden Slippers (Oh Dem Golden Slippers)
Hand Me Down My Walking Cane
In the Evening by the Moonlight

Henry Blossom Songs
Because You're You
Every Day is Ladies Day with Me
In Old New York (The Streets of New York)
Kiss Me Again (If I Were on the Stage)
Love is Best of All
Moonbeams
Neapolitan Love Song
Thine Alone
When You're Away (Dear)

Johannes Brahms Selections
Gaudeamus Igitur
Hungarian Dance No.5
Lullaby (Wiegenlied)
Symphony No.1

J. Keirn Brennan Songs
Dear Little Boy of Mine
Goodbye, Good Luck, God Bless You
Ireland Is Ireland to Me
Let the Rest of the World Go By
Little Bit of Heaven, Sure They Call It Ireland, A

Alfred Bryan Songs
Come, Josephine, in My Flying Machine
I Didn't Raise My Boy to Be a Soldier
Peg o' My Heart
Sweet Little Buttercup

Henry/Harry Thacker (H.T.) Burleigh Songs
Come Unto Me
Deep River
Go Down Moses
In the Great Somewhere
Little David Play on Your Harp
Little Mother of Mine
Nobody Knows the Trouble I've Seen
Oh, Didn't It Rain
Sometimes I Feel Like a Motherless Child
Steal Away
Swing Low, Sweet Chariot
'Tis Me Oh Lord, Standin' in de Need of Pray'r

Fréderic Chopin Selections
Fantaisie-Impromptu
Funeral March (Marche Funèbre)
Minute Waltz
Nocturne Op.9, No. 2
Polonaise in A-flat
Polonaise Militaire
Prelude

Grant Clarke Songs
Everything is Peaches Down in Georgia
He's a Devil in His Own Home Town
Ragtime Cowboy Joe
Second Hand Rose
When You're in Love with Someone Who Is Not in Love with You

George M. Cohan Songs
Give My Regards to Broadway
Harrigan
I Am the Yankee Doodle Boy
Mary's a Grand Old Name
Over There
You're a Grand Old Flag

Claude Debussy Selections
Clair de Lune
Golliwogg's Cake Walk
Mer, La
Reverie

Bud (B.G.) De Sylva Songs
April Showers
Avalon
I'll Build a Stairway to Paradise
Kiss in the Dark, A
Look for the Silver Lining
Whip-Poor-Will
You Ain't Heard Nothing Yet

Walter Donaldson
Carolina in the Morning
Daughter of Rosie O'Grady, The
How You ('Ya) Going to Keep 'Em Down on the Farm After They've Seen Paree?
My Buddy
My Mammy

Antonin Dvorák Selections
Humoresque
Largo
New World Symphony
Slavonic Dances
Songs My Mother Taught Me

Gus Edwards Songs
By the Light of the Silvery Moon
In My Merry Oldsmobile
School Days
Sunbonnet Sue

Raymond B. Egan Songs
Ain't We Got Fun
Bimini Bay
Japanese Sandman, The
Some Sunday Morning
Till We Meet Again (Smile the While You Kiss Me Sad Adieu)
Where the Morning Glories Grow

Fred Fisher Songs
Chicago (That Toddling Town)
Come, Josephine, in My Flying Machine
Dardanella
Ireland Must Be Heaven, for My Mother Came from There
Peg o' My Heart
There's a Broken Heart for Every Light on Broadway
They Go Wild Simply Wild Over Me

Stephen Foster Songs
Beautiful Dreamer
Camptown Races, De
Jeannie with the Light Brown Hair
Massa's in de Cold (Cold) Ground
My Old Kentucky Home
Nelly Bly
Nelly Was a Lady

Oh! Susanna
Old Dog Tray
Old Black Joe
Way Down Upon the Swanee River (Old Folks at Home)

Rudolf Friml Songs
Giannina Mia
Katinka
L'Amour-Toujours-L'Amour (Love Everlasting)
Sometime
Sympathy

Gilbert & Sullivan Selections
Come, Friends, Who Plough the Sea
He is an Englishman
I'm Called Little Buttercup
Modern Major General
My Object All Sublime
Three Little Maids from School
Wand'ring Minstrel, A
We Sail the Ocean Blue

Edvard Grieg Selections
Concerto for Piano
In the Hall of the Mountain King
March of the Dwarfs
Peer Gynt

George Frederick Handel Selections
Bourrée (from "Water Music")
Bourrée (from "Royal Fireworks Music")
Hallelujah Chorus
Messiah
Royal Fireworks Music
Water Music

W. C. Handy Songs
Beale Street
Joe Turner Blues

Memphis Blues, The
St. Louis Blues

Otto Harbach Songs

Cuddle Up a Little Closer, Lovey Mine
Every Little Movement (Has a meaning all its own)
Giannina Mia
Katinka
Love Nest, The
Sympathy

Victor Herbert Songs

Ah! Sweet Mystery of Life
Because You're You
Every Day is Ladies' Day with Me
Gypsy Love Song (Slumber on)
I Might Be Your Once-In-A-While
If I Were on the Stage (Kiss Me Again)
I'm Falling in Love with Someone
In Old New York (The Streets of New York)
Italian Street Song
Kiss in the Dark, A
Love is the Best of All
March of the Toys
Moonbeams
Neapolitan Love Song
Sweethearts
Thine Alone
Toyland
Tramp! Tramp! Tramp! (Along the highway)
When You're Away (Dear)
You Belong to Me

William Jerome Songs

And the Green Grass Grew All Around
Bedelia
Chinatown, My Chinatown
Row, Row, and Row (And then he'd)
That Old Irish Mother of Mine

Howard Johnson Songs

Ireland Must Be Heaven, For My Mother Came from There
M-O-T-H-E-R (A Word That Means the World to Me)
There's a Broken Heart for Every Light on Broadway
What Do You Want to Make Those Eyes at Me For

Scott Joplin Songs

Breeze from Alabama, A
Chrysanthemum, The
Easy Winners, The
Entertainer, The
Maple Leaf Rag
Palm Leaf Rag
Reflection Rag
Searchlight Rag
Solace
Sycamore, The
Weeping Willow

Gus Kahn Songs

Ain't We Got Fun
Bimini Bay
Carolina in the Morning
I Wish I Had a Girl
Memories
My Buddy
Pretty Baby
Some Sunday Morning
Toot, Toot, Tootsie (Goo' Bye)
Where the Morning Glories Grow
You Ain't Heard Nothing Yet

Jerome Kern Songs

Babes in the Wood
Have a Heart
How'd You Like to Spoon with Me?
Look for the Silver Lining
Old-Fashioned Wife, An
Sally

They Didn't Believe Me
Till the Clouds Roll By
Whip-Poor-Will
You Know and I Know (and we both understand)

Sam M. Lewis Songs

Daddy Long Legs
How You ('Ya) Going to Keep 'Em Down On the Farm
       After They've Seen Paree?
I'm All Bound 'Round with the Mason-Dixon Line
My Little Girl
My Mammy
My Mother's Rosary
Rock-a-Bye Your Baby with a Dixie Melody
When You're a Long, Long Way from Home

Ballard MacDonald Songs

Beautiful Ohio
Indiana (Back Home Again in)
I've Got the Time—I've Got the Place, but It's Hard to Find the Girl
Parade of the Wooden Soldiers
Rose of Washington Square
Trail of the Lonesome Pine, The

Joseph McCarthy Songs

(In My Sweet Little) Alice Blue Gown
I'm Always Chasing Rainbows
Ireland Must Be Heaven, for My Mother Came from There
They Go Wild Simply Wild Over Me
What Do You Want to Make Those Eyes at Me For
You Made Me Love You (I didn't want to do it)

Felix Mendelssohn Selections

Elijah
Hark! The Herald Angels Sing
Spring Song
Wedding March (Recessional)

George W. Meyer Songs
Everything is Peaches Down in Georgia
For Me and My Gal
My Mother's Rosary
When You're a Long, Long Way from Home

W.A. Mozart Selections
Cosi Fan Tutte
Don Giovanni
Jupiter Symphony
Kleine Nachtmusik, Eine
Magic Flute, The (Die Zauberflöte)
Nozze di Figaro, Le

Stanley Murphy Songs
Be My Little Baby Bumble Bee
Oh! How She Could Yacki, Hacki, Wicki, Wacki, Woo
On the 5:15
Put on Your Old Grey Bonnet

Al Piantadosi Songs
Baby Shoes
I Didn't Raise My Boy to Be a Soldier
If You Had All the World and Its Gold
When You're in Love with Someone Who Is Not in Love with You

Giacomo Puccini Selections
Madama Butterfly
Musetta's Waltz
Un Bel Di ·
Vissi d'Arte

Sigmund Romberg Songs
Auf Wiedersehen
Fascination
Song of Love
When Hearts Are Young
Will You Remember (sweetheart)

Jean Schwartz Songs
Bedelia
Chinatown, My Chinatown
I'm All Bound 'Round with the Mason-Dixon Line
Rock-a-Bye Your Baby with a Dixie Melody

John Philip Sousa Selections
Bride Elect, The
Capitan, El
Gladiator, The
Hands Across the Sea
King Cotton
Last Days of Pompeii, The
Manhattan Beach March
New York Hippodrome March
Semper Fidelis
Stars and Stripes Forever
Thunderer, The
Washington Post March

Johann Strauss, Jr., Selections
Artist's Life
Blue Danube, The
Du und Du
Emperor Waltz (Kaiser-Walzer)
Fledermaus, Die
Tales from the Vienna Woods
Vienna Life (Wiener Blut)
Wine, Women and Song

Andrew B. Sterling Songs
Meet Me in St. Louis, Louis
On a Sunday Afternoon
Wait Till the Sun Shines, Nellie
We're Going Over
When My Baby Smiles at Me

Peter I. Tchaikovsky Selections
1812 Overture
Marche Slave

The Nutcracker Suite
Piano Concerto No.1
Sleeping Beauty
Swan Lake
Waltz of the Flowers

Giuseppe Verdi Selections
Aida
Anvil Chorus
Forza del Destino, La
Otello
Rigoletto
Traviata, La
Triumphal March

Albert von Tilzer Songs
Give Me the Moonlight, Give Me the Girl
I Used to Love You, But It's All Over Now
I'll Be With You in Apple Blossom Time
My Little Girl
Oh! By Jingo, Oh! By Gee, You're the Only Girl for Me
Oh! How She Could Yacki, Hacki, Wicki, Wacki, Woo
Put Your Arms Around Me, Honey (Hold me tight)
Take Me Out to the Ball Game

Harry von Tilzer Songs
And the Green Grass Grew All Around
Bird in a Gilded Cage, A
I Want a Girl (Just Like the Girl That Married Dear Old Dad)
In the Sweet Bye and Bye
On Sunday Afternoon
That Old Irish Mother of Mine
Wait Till the Sun Shines, Nellie

Richard Wagner Selections
Götterdämmerung
Liebestod
March, from Tannhaüser
Rheingold, Das
Ride of the Valkyries
Ring Des Nibelungen, Der

Siegfried
Tristan und Isolde
Walküre, Die
Wedding March (Here comes the bride)

Richard A. Whiting Songs
Ain't We Got Fun
Bimini Bay
It's Tulip Time in Holland
Japanese Sandman, The
Smile the While You Kiss Me Sad Adieu (Till We Meet Again)
Some Sunday Morning
Where the Morning Glories Grow

Joe Young Songs
Along the Rocky Road to Dublin
Daddy Long Legs
How You ('Ya) Going to Keep 'Em Down on the Farm After They've Seen Paree?
I'm All Bound 'Round with the Mason-Dixon Line
My Mammy
Rock-a-Bye Your Baby With a Dixie Melody
Yaaka Hula Hickey Dula

Rida Johnson Young Songs
Ah! Sweet Mystery of Life
I'm Falling in Love with Someone
Italian Street Song
Mother Machree
Sometime
Tramp! Tramp! Tramp! (Along the highway)
Will You Remember (sweetheart)

Composers and Their Birth and Death Dates

For information about how the birth and death dates of the composers were researched, please see the section, *Dating of Songs and Birth and Death Dates of Composers* in the introduction. Because most countries have no national death registries, we have had to use secondary sources to determine these dates. <u>While we have taken as much care as possible in researching these dates, we cannot warrant their accuracy.</u> The section entitled "Explanation of Symbols and Notations Used in Conjunction With Dates," under *Dating of Songs*, explains the meaning of notations like: (1893-1942 A).

A

Maurice Abrahams (1883-1931 A)

Adolphe-Charles Adam (1803-1856)

A. Emmett Adams (? -1938 P)

Frank R. Adams (1883/84-1963)

Sarah F. Adams (1805-1834)

Milton Ager (1893-1979)

Fred E. Ahlert (1892-1953 A)

Kenneth J. Alford (pseudonym – see Major Frederick J. Ricketts)

Thomas S. Allen

Henry W. Armstrong (1879-1951)

Thomas Augustine Arne (1710-1778)

George Asaf (1880-1951)

Harold R. Atteridge (1886-1938)

Nat D. Ayer (1887-1952)

B

J.S. Bach (1685-1750)

E.E. Bagley (1857-1922)

Theodore Baker (185?-1934)

Ernest R. Ball (1878-1927)

J. Barbier (1822/25-1901)

Rev. Sabine Baring-Gould (1834-1924)

J. (Joseph) Barnby (1838-1896)

F.J. Barnes

Billy Baskette (1884-1949 A)

Katharine Lee Bates (1859-1929)

Nora Bayes-Norworth (1880-1928)

Thomas Haynes Bayly (1797-1839)

Carl Beck (1886-1965)

Ludwig van Beethoven (1770-1827)

Reverend George Bennard (1873-1958)

David Berg (1892-1944 A)

Irving Berlin (1888-1989)

Felix Bernard (1897-1944)

Paul Bernard

Heinrich Berté (1857/58-1924)

C. Clifton Bingham (1859-1913)

Henry Bishop (1786-1855)

Georges Bizet (1838-1875)

James M. Black

Johnny S. Black (1891-1936)

Jay Blackton (1909-1994 A)

Eubie Blake (1883-1983 A)

James W. Blake (1862-1935)

James A. Bland (1854-1911)

Henry Blossom (1866-1919)

A. Boito (1842-1918)

Heinz Bolten-Bäckers

Horatius Bonar (1808-1889)

Alexander Borodin (1833-1887)

Louis Bourgeois (1510?-15??)

Frederick V. Bowers (1874-1961 A)

Euday L. Bowman (1887-1949)

Philip Braham (?-1934 P)

Johannes Brahms (1833-1897)

John W. Bratton (1867-1947 A)

J. Keirn Brennan (1873-1948)

Monty C. Brice (1891-1962)

Mary D. Brine (1836-1925)

James Brockman (1886/87-1967)

Phillips Brooks (1835-1893)

Shelton Brooks (1886-1975 A)

Albert H. Brown

A. Seymour Brown (1885-1947 A)

Lew Brown (1893-1958)

Walter H. Brown

Alfred Bryan (1871-1958 A)

Vincent P. Bryan (1883-1937)

J. Tim Bryman (1879-1946 A)

Gene Buck (1885-1957)

Richard Henry Buck (1870-1956 A)

Henry/Harry Thacker (H.T.) Burleigh (1866/86-1949)

Ernie Burnett (1884-1959)

Robert Burns (1759-1796)

James Henry Burris

Henry Busse (1894-1955)

Gen. Daniel O. Butterfield (1831-1901)

James A. Butterfield (1837-1891)

Robert Byrd (1930-1990 B)

C

Charles Wakefield Cadman (1881-1946)

Irving Caesar (1895-   )

Anne Caldwell (1867-1936)

John Baptiste Calkin (1827-1905)

J. Will Callahan (1874-1946)

Salvatore Cammarano (1801-1852)

Frank Campbell

Evelyn Cannon (1880-1949)

Hughie Cannon (1877-1912)

Victor Capoul (1839-1924)

Placide Cappeau (1808-1877)

G. Capurro (1859-1920 S)

Bob Carleton (1896-1956 A)

Monte Carlo (1883-1967 A)

M. Carré (? -1872)

Harry Carroll (1892-1962)

Ivan Caryll (1860/61-1921)

J.M. Cavanass

Emmanuel Chabrier (1841-1894)

Henry Chalfont (1882-1953)

Annie Chambers-Ketchum (1824?-1904)

Arthur Chapman

Jacques Charles (1882-1971)

Edward Chevalier (1886-1968)

Fréderic Chopin (1810-1849)

E.P. Christy (1815-1862)

Sidney Clare (1892-1972 A)

Grant Clarke (1891-1931)

Jeremiah Clarke (1674-1707)

Edward B. Claypoole (1883-1952 A)

N.J. Clesi

Will D. Cobb (1876-1930)

Richard Coburn (pseudonym – see Frank D. de Long)

George M. Cohan (1878-1942)

Robert (Bob) Cole (1869-1911)

Edward E. (Zez) Confrey (1895-1971)

Con Conrad (pseudonym - see Conrad K. Dober))

Charles Converse (1832-1918)

Leonard Cooke (? -1919 P)

Sam Coslow (1902-1982)

Bartley Costello (1871-1941)

T. Cottrau (1827-1879)

Henry Creamer (1879-1930)

Effie I. Crockett

William Croft (1678-1727)

Catherine Chisholm Cushing (1874-1952)

D

Harry Dacre (? -1922 P)

Joseph M. Daly (1888-1968 A)

Charles N. Daniels (1878-1943)

H.P. Danks (1834-1903)

Lorenzo Da Ponte (1749-1838)

Lee David (1891-1978 A)

Benny Davis (1895-1979)

Claude Debussy (1862-1918)

Ernesto de Curtis (1875-1937 S)

Giovanni Battista de Curtis (1860-1926 S)

Felice de Giardini (1716-1796)

Reginald De Koven (1859-1920)

Countess Ada Goudard de Lachau (?-1940)

Tom Delaney

J. de Lau Lusignan

Leo Delibes (1836-1891)

Frank D. de Long (1886-1952)

Arthur de Lulli

Lucien Denni (1886/87-1947)

Luigi Denza (1846-1922)

Bud (B.G.) De Sylva (1895-1950)

Guy d'Hardelot (? -1936 P)

E. di Capua (1864-1917 S)

William A. Dillon (1877-1966)

William Chatterton Dix (1837-1898)

Conrad K. Dober (1891-1938)

Walter Donaldson (1893-1947)

Dorothy Donnelly (1880-1928 A)

Walter Donovan (1888-1964 A)

William Douglas

Paul Dresser (1857-1906)

Paul Dukas (1865-1935)

Antonin Dvorák (1841-1904)

John Sullivan Dwight (1813/18-1893)

John Bacchus Dykes (1823-1876)

E

D. Eardley-Wilmot

Mary Earl (pseudonym - see Robert A. King)

Nelle Richmond Eberhart (1871-1944)

Harry Edelheit (1891-1955 A)

Gus Edwards (1879-1945)

Raymond B. Egan (1890-1952)

Edward Elgar (1857-1934)

Zo Elliott (1891-1964)

Ida Emerson

Daniel Decatur Emmett (1815-1904)

Ernie Erdman (1879-1946)

D.A. Esrom (pseudonym - see Theodora Morse)

George Evans (1870-1915)

F

Frederick Faber (1814-1863)

John Fawcett (1739/40-1817)

John S. Fearis (1867-1932)

Arthur Fields (1888-1953)

Ted Fiorito (1900-1971)

Fred Fisher (1875-1942)

Neville Fleeson (1887-1945 A)

Lucy Fletcher

Judith Fontana (1871-1920)

Lena Guilbert Ford

Stephen Foster (1826-1864)

Arthur Francis (pseudonym - see Ira Gershwin)

Martin Fried (1923-1980 A)

Anatole Friedland (1881-1938 A)

Leo Friedman (1869-1927 A)

W. Friedrich

Cliff Friend (1893-1974)

Rudolf Friml (1879-1972)

Julius Fucik (1872-1916)

Douglas Furber (1885/86-1961)

Nilson Fysher (? -1931 P)

G

Ed Gallagher

Percy Gaunt (1852-1896)

Adam Geibel (1855-1933)

R. Genée (1823-1895)

Richard H. Gerard (1876-1948)

George Gershwin (1898-1937)

Ira Gershwin (1896-1983)

A. Ghislanzoni (1824-1893)

Giuseppe Giacosa (1847-1906)

A. Harrington Gibbs (1896-1956)

George L. Giefer

Harry Gifford (? -1960 P)

L. Wolfe Gilbert (1886-1970)

W.S. Gilbert (1836-1911)

Patrick Sarsfield Gilmore (1829-1892)

John Gilroy (? -1979 A)

Benjamin Godard (1849-1895)

E. Ray Goetz (1886-1954)

John L. Golden (1874-1955)

Alfred (Al) Goodman (1890-1972)

Joe Goodwin (1889-1943 A)

Walter Goodwin (1889-1966 A)

Ross Gorman

Charles Gounod (1818-1893)

George Graff, Jr. (1886-1973)

Gerald Grafton

Roger Graham (1885-1938)

Bert Grant (1878-1951 A)

William B. Gray (? -1932)

Eddie Green (1901-1950)

Charles Greene (1874-1937)

Schuyler Greene (1880-1927 A)

Clifford Grey (1887-1941)

Joe Grey (1879/80-1956)

Edvard Grieg (1843-1907)

Ferde Grofé (1892-1972)

Bernie Grossman (1885-1951 A)

Edmund L. Gruber (1879-1941)

Franz Gruber (1787-1863)

Albert Gumble (1883-1946 A)

H

C. Haffner

Clyde Hager (1886-1944 A)

Sarah Josepha Hale (1788-1879)

L. Halévy (1834-1908)

Ed Haley (pseudonym - see Robert A. King)

Benjamin R. Hanby (1833-1867)

George Frederick Handel (1685-1759)

W.C. Handy (1873-1958)

James F. Hanley (1892-1942 A)

Bert Hanlon (1890-1972 A)

Otto Harbach (1873-1963)

Charles K. Harris (1867-1930)

Annie Fortescue Harrison (1851-1944)

Thomas Hastings (1784-1872)

Alice Hawthorne (pseudonym - see Septimus Winner)

Franz Joseph Haydn (1732-1809)

Joseph Hayden (? -1937)

Bobby Heath (1889/90-1952)

Reginald Heber (1783-1826)

Anna Held (1873?-1918)

H.F. Hemy (1818-1888)

S.R. Henry

Victor Herbert (1859-1924)

Adolf Heyduk (1835-1923)

William (Billy) Higgins

Brewster Higley (1823-1911)

Louis A. Hirsch (1887-1924)

John H. Hopkins (1820-1891)

Charles Horwitz (1864-1938)

Karl Hoschna (1877-1911)

Will M. Hough (1882-1962)

Joseph E. Howard (1878-1961)

Julia Ward Howe (1819-1910)

Charles H. Hoyt (1860-1900)

Raymond Hubbell (1879-1954)

Engelbert Humperdinck (1854-1921)

I

Luigi Illica (1857-1919)

I. Ivanovici (1845-1902)

J

Tony Jackson (1876-1921)

Carrie Jacobs-Bond (1862-1946)

Charles Jennens (1700-1773)

William Jerome (1865-1932)

Léon Jessel (1871-1942)

Billy Johnson

Buster Johnson

George W. Johnson (1839-1917)

Howard Johnson (1887-1941 A)

James Weldon Johnson (1871-1938)

J. Rosamond Johnson (1873-1954)

Al Jolson (1886-1950)

Ben Jonson (1572-1637)

Scott Joplin (1868-1919)

Jack Judge (1878-1938)

K

J. K.

Grace LeBoy Kahn (1891-1983 A)

Gus Kahn (1886-1941)

Henry Kailimai

Kurt Kaiser

Emmerich Kalman (1882-1953 A)

Bert Kalmar (1884-1947)

John William Kellette (pseudonym for 2-3 composers - see James Brockman, James Kendis, Nathaniel H. Vincent)

Daniel Kelley

Jaan/Jean Kenbrovin (pseudonym - see Nathaniel H. Vincent)

James Kendis (1883-1946 A)

Jimmy M. Kennedy (1902-1984)

Jerome Kern (1885-1945)

Albert William Ketelbey (1875-1959)

Francis Scott Key (1779-1843)

Gilbert Keyes (pseudonym - see Gus Kahn)

George Kiallmark

Joyce Kilmer (1886-1918)

Robert A. King (1862/63-1932)

Stoddard King (1889-1933 A)

Rudyard Kipling (1865-1936)

Walter Kittredge (1834-1905)

Lou Klein (1888-1945 A)

Joseph P. Knight (1812-1887)

Fritz Kreisler (1875-1962)

L

Paul Lacome

Arthur J. Lamb (1870-1928)

Louis Lambert (pseudonym - see Patrick Sarsfield Gilmore)

J. Bodewalt Lampe (1869-1929 A)

Arthur Lange (1889-1956 A)

Edward Laska (1884-1959 A)

Harry Lauder (1870-1950)

Charles B. Lawlor (1852-1925)

Turner Layton (1894-1978)

Alfred Lee

Franz Lehar (1870-1948)

Fred W. Leigh (? -1924 P)

Bert Leighton (1877-1964 A)

Frank Leighton

F. Lemaire

Jean Lenox

Eddie Leonard (1875-1941 A)

Ruggiero Leoncavallo (1858-1919)

Edgar Leslie (1885-1976)

Will Letters (? -1938 P)

Roger Lewis (1885-1948 A)

Sam M. Lewis (1885-1959)

Ted Lewis (1891/92-1971)

George Leybourne (? -1884 P)

Thurlow Lieurance (1878-1963)

Princess Liliuokalani (1838-1917)

Paul Lincke (1867-1946)

Franz Liszt (1811-1886)

Eugene Lockhart (1891-1957 A)

Frederic Knight Logan (1871-1928)

Hermann Lohr (1871-1943)

H.W. Longfellow (1807-1882)

Samuel Lover (1797-1868)

Clarence Lucas (1866-1947)

Martin Luther (1483-1546)

Henry Francis Lyte (1793-1847)

M

Harry MacCarthy

Ballard MacDonald (1882-1935 A)

Glen MacDonough (1870-1924 A)

Edward A. MacDowell (1861-1908)

Thomas Mack (1880-1943)

Alexander Campbell Mackenzie (1847-1935)

Edward Madden (1877-1952)

Jack Mahoney (1882-1945)

David Mallet (1705?-1765)

F.D. Marchetti (? -1940 P)

Earnest Maresca (1939-   )

Alfred Margis (1874-1913)

Godfrey Marks

Henry I. Marshall (1883-1958)

Easthope Martin (1882-1925 A)

Lowell Mason (1792-1872)

Charles McCarron (1891-1919 A)

Joseph McCarthy (1885-1943)

Junie McCree (1865-1918)

William J. McKenna (1881-1950)

F.W. Meacham (1850/56-1909)

H. Meilhac (1831-1897)

Fred Meinken (1883-1958)

Tom Mellor (? -1926 P)

Felix Mendelssohn (1809-1847)

Theodore A. Metz (1848-1936)

George W. Meyer (1884-1959)

Giacomo Meyerbeer (1791-1864)

Richard Milburn

C. Austin Miles (1868-1946)

Irving Mills (1894-1985)

Kerry Mills (1869-1948)

Joseph Mohr (1792-1848)

J.L. Molloy (1837-1909)

James V. Monaco (1885-1945)

Lionel Monk (1836-1880)

William Henry Monk (1823-1889)

James Montgomery (1771-1854)

John Charles Moore (? -1938 P)

Thomas Moore (1779-1852)

Carey Morgan (1885-1960 A)

Theodora Morse (1890-1953)

Theodore F. Morse (1873/74-1924)

Ferdinand "Jelly Roll" Morton (1885/90-1941)

Moya (pseudonym - see Harold Vicars)

W.A. Mozart (1756-1791)

Gus Mueller

Lewis F. Muir (1884-1950)

Bill Munro (1892-1969)

Eddie Munson

C.W. Murphy (? -1913 P)

Stanley Murphy (1875-1919 A)

James Ramsey Murray (1841-1905)

Modeste Mussorgsky (1839-1881)

N

Hans G. Naegeli (1773-1836)

Rev. John Mason Neale (1818-1866)

John Neat (? -1949 A & P)

Marshall Neilan

Ethelbert Nevin (1862-1901)

John Henry Newman

Eddie Newton

Eileen Newton

Michael Nolan

George A. Norton (1880-1923)

Jack Norworth (1879-1959)

Ivor Novello (1893-1951)

Maude Nugent (187?-1958)

O

Frederick Oakeley (1802-1880)

Shamus O'Connor

Charles O'Donnell

Jacques Offenbach (1819-1880)

Fiske O'Hara (1878-1945)

Geoffrey O'Hara (1882-1967)

Chauncey Olcott (1858-1932)

Abe Olman (1888-1984)

D. Onivas (pseudonym – see Domenico Savino)

Harold Orlob (1883/85-1982 A)

Meta Orred

W. Benton Overstreet

Albert Owen (1876-1935)

P

Johann Pachelbel (1653-1706)

Ignace Paderewski (1860-1941)

Herman Paley (1879-1955)

John E. Palmer

F.A. Partichela

Richard W. Pascoe (1888-1968 A)

John Howard Payne (1791-1852)

Eugene Pearson (birth date?-living per BMI)

Gilbert Peele (1874-1942)

Arthur A. Penn (1875/76-1941)

A. Pestalozza (1851-1934 S)

Henry E. Pether (? -1932 P)

Henry W. Petrie (1857-1925)

Dave Peyton

Estelle Philleo

Al Piantadosi (1884-1955)

F.M. Piave (1810-1876)

J. Pierpont (1822-1893)

Maceo Pinkard (1897-1962)

Armand J. Piron (1888-1943 A)

Channing Pollock (1880-1946)

Amilcare Ponchielli (1834-1886)

Cole Porter (1891/92-1964)

Jessie Brown Pounds (1861-1921)

Felix Powell (1878-1942)

Adelaide A. Proctor (1825-1864)

Arthur Pryor (1870-1942)

Giacomo Puccini (1858-1924)

Henry Purcell (1659-1695)

W.T. Purdy (1882-1918/19)

Katharine E. Purvis

R

Dave Radford (1884-1968 A)

James Ryder Randall (1839-1908)

Oscar (Otto) Rasbach (1889-1975)

Maurice Ravel (1875-1937)

Lillian Ray (pseudonym - see John Neat)

L.H. Redner (1831-1908)

Dave Reed, Jr. (1872/73-1946)

Billy Reeves (1943 -   )

C. Francis Reisner (1887-1962 A)

Eben E. Rexford (184?-1916)

Herbert Reynolds (1867-1933)

Gitz Rice (1891-1947)

Seymour Rice

Major Frederick J. Ricketts (1881-1945)

Nikolai Rimsky-Korsakov (1844-1908)

Dave Ringle (1895-1965)

Harold Robé (1881-1946 A)

Lee S. Roberts (1884-1949)

J. Russel Robinson (1892-1963)

Lilla Cayley Robinson

Julian Robledo (1887-1940)

Robert Cameron Rogers (1862-1912)

Sigmund Romberg (1887-1951)

George Frederick Root (1820-1895)

Ed Rose (1875-1935)

Vincent Rose (1880-1944)

William (Billy) Rose (1899-1966)

Monroe Rosenfeld (1861/62-1918)

Adrian Ross (1859-1933)

Gioacchino Rossini (1792-1868)

Claude Rouget de Lisle (1760-1836)

Anton Rubinstein (1829/30-1894)

Harry Ruby (1895-1974)

James J. Russell (? -1900 M)

Dan Russo (1925-1956 A)

Ben Ryan (1887/92-1968 A)

S

Camille Saint-Saëns (1835-1921)

Alma Sanders (1882-1956 A)

James Sanderson (1769-1841)

Lester Santly (1895-1983)

V. Sardou (1831-1908)

Domenico Savino (1882-1973)

Henry J. Sayers (1855-1932)

E. Schikaneder (1751-1812)

Friedrich Schiller (1759-1805)

John Schonberger (1892-1983 A)

Malvin Schonberger

Franz Schubert (1797-1828)

Robert Schumann (1810-1856)

Jean Schwartz (1878-1956)

Clinton Scollard (1860-1932)

Clement Scott (1841-1904)

Lady John Scott

Maurice Scott (? -1933 P)

Walter Scott (1771-1832)

Vincent Scotto (1876-1952)

Edmund H. Sears (1810-1876)

T. Lawrence Seibert

Ernest Seitz

James Royce Shannon (1881-1946 A)

Al Shean (1868-1949)

Ren Shields (1868-1913)

Jean Sibelius (1865-1957)

Lao Silesu (? -1953 P)

Louis Silvers (1889-1954)

Armand Silvestre (1837/8-1901)

L.W. Simpson (1811-1883)

John Lang Sinclair

Noble Sissle (1889-1975 A)

Henry Smart (1813-1879)

Chris Smith (1879-1949)

Harry B. Smith (1860-1936)

John Stafford Smith (1750-1836)

Laura Rountree Smith (1876-1924)

Robert B. Smith (1875-1951)

Samuel Francis Smith (1808-1895)

Geoffrey Smitham (1888-1952)

Ted Snyder (1881-1965)

Alfred Solman (1868-1937)

John Philip Sousa (1854-1932)

Oley Speaks (1874-1948)

Otis Spencer (1890-1958 A)

Jonathan E. Spilman (1812-1896)

Louis Spohr (1784-1859)

John J. Stamford

Stanislaus Stange (?-1917)

Frank L. Stanton (1857-1927)

Richard Starfield (1884-1957)

Andrew B. Sterling (1874-1955)

Byron D. Stokes (1886-1974 A)

G.H. Stover

Oscar Straus (1870-1954)

Johann Strauss, Jr. (1825-1899)

Richard Strauss (1864-1949)

John Stromberg (1853-1902)

Arthur Sullivan (1842-1900)

Joseph J. Sullivan

Harry O. Sutton

T

John Talbot (1847-1905)

Arthur F. Tate (? -1950 A & P)

Helen Taylor (?-1943)

Tell Taylor (1876-1937)

Peter I. Tchaikovsky (1840-1893)

Alfred Tennyson (1809-1892)

Dorothy Terriss (pseudonym - see Theodora Morse)

Edward Teschemacher (? -1940 P)

Jimmie Thomas (birth date?-living per BMI)

James Thomson (1700-1748)

James Thornton (1861-1938)

Harry Tierney (1890-1965)

Carlo Tiochet

Theodore Moses Tobani (1855-1933)

Augustus Montague Toplady (1740-1778)

William Tracey (1893-1957 A)

Huntley Trevor (? -1943 P)

G. Turco

V

Egbert van Alstyne (1882-1951)

Gottfried van Swieten (1733-1803)

Maurice Vaucaire (186?-1918)

Giuseppe Verdi (1813-1901)

F. Dudleigh Vernor (1892-1974 A)

Harold Vicars (? -1922)

A.G. Villoldo (? - 1919 SA)

Nathaniel H. Vincent (1889/90-1979 A)

Antonio Vivaldi (1678-1741)

Friedrich von Flotow (1812/13-1883)

Franz von Suppé (1819-1895)

Albert von Tilzer (1878-1956)

Harry von Tilzer (1872-1946)

W

John Francis Wade (1710/11-1786)

Richard Wagner (1813-1883)

Emile Waldteufel (1837-1915)

James J. Walker (1881-1946 A)

Oliver G. Wallace (1887-1963 A)

Charles B. Ward (1865-1917)

Samuel Augustus Ward (1847/8-1903)

Charles Warfield

Harry Warren (1893-1981)

Isaac Watts (1674-1748)

Frederick Edward Weatherly (1848-1929)

Harold Weeks (1893-1967 A)

Pete Wendling (1888-1974 A)

Percy Wenrich (1880/87-1952)

Charles Wesley (1707-1788)

Eugene West (1883-1949 A)

Thomas P. Westendorf (1848-1923)

R.P. Weston (1878-1936)

Adelheid Wette (1858-1916)

Francis Wheeler

Paul Whiteman (1890-1967)

Richard A. Whiting (1891-1938)

Beth Slater Whitson (1879-1930)

General Beauregard Wilks (1824-1875)

Mrs. Emma C. Hart Willard (1787-1870)

Albert Willemetz (1887-1964)

Clarence Williams (1893/98-1965)

Harry Williams

Harry H. Williams (1879-1922)

Spencer Williams (1889-1965)

W.R. Williams (1867-1954 A)

Richard Storrs Willis (1819-1900)

D. Eardley-Wilmot

Jeanne Wilson (1865-1938)

Phillip Wingate

Joseph E. Winner (1837-1918)

Septimus Winner (1827-1902)

P.G. Wodehouse (1881-1975)

Charles Wood (1807-1876)

Cyrus Wood (1889-1942)

Haydn Wood (? -1959 P)

Leo Wood (1882-1929)

Samuel Woodworth (1784/85-1842)

Henry Clay Work (1832-1884)

Y

Jack Yellen (1892-1991 A)

Joe Young (1889-1939)

John Freeman Young (1820-1885)

Rida Johnson Young (1869-1926)

Sebastian Yradier (1809-1865)

Maurice Yvain (1891-1965)

Z

Charles A. Zimmerman (1861/62-1916)

Published by
The BZ/Rights Stuff, Inc.
a subsidiary of BZ/Rights & Permissions, Inc.
121 West 27th Street, Suite 901
New York, NY 10001
Phone: (212) 924-3000
Fax: (212) 924-2525
Email: info@bzrights.com
Website: www.bzrights.com